Organized Chaos

K. H. Burkett

Copyright © 2018 K. H. Burkett

All rights reserved.

ISBN: 1727650654
ISBN-13: 978-1727650655

DEDICATION

This book is dedicated to everyone that finds beauty in the chaos in life. When you learn to embrace the crazy you find that things can be quiet lovely.

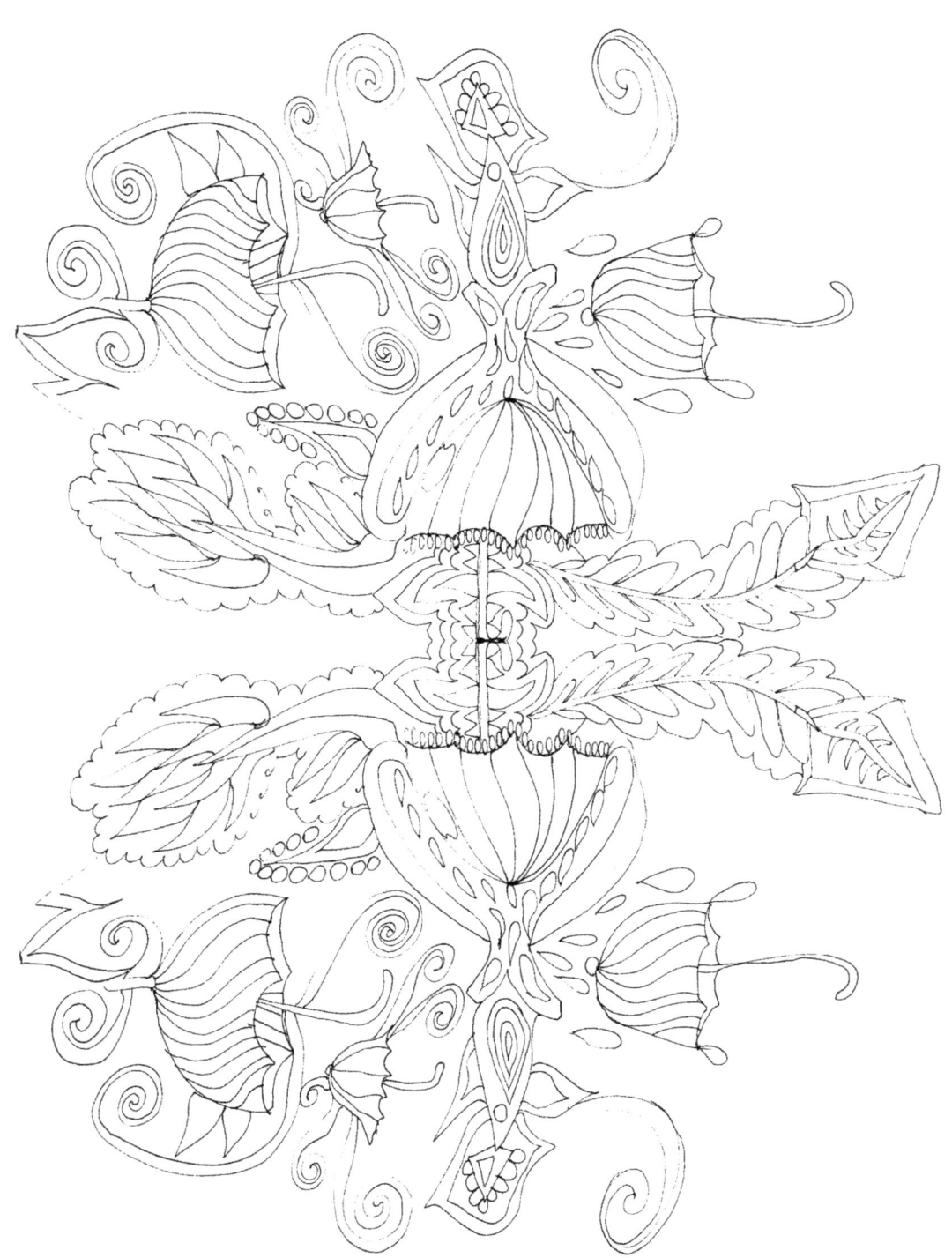

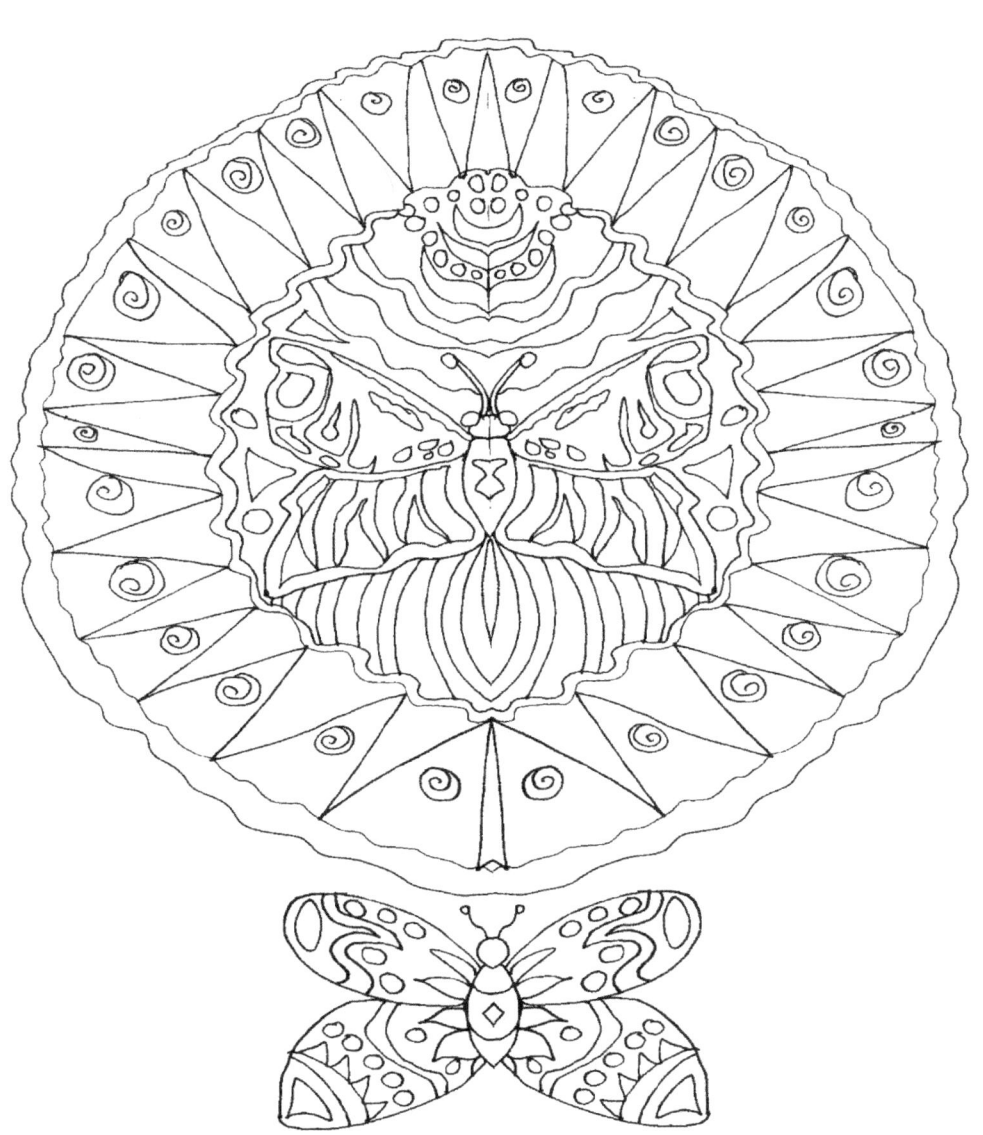

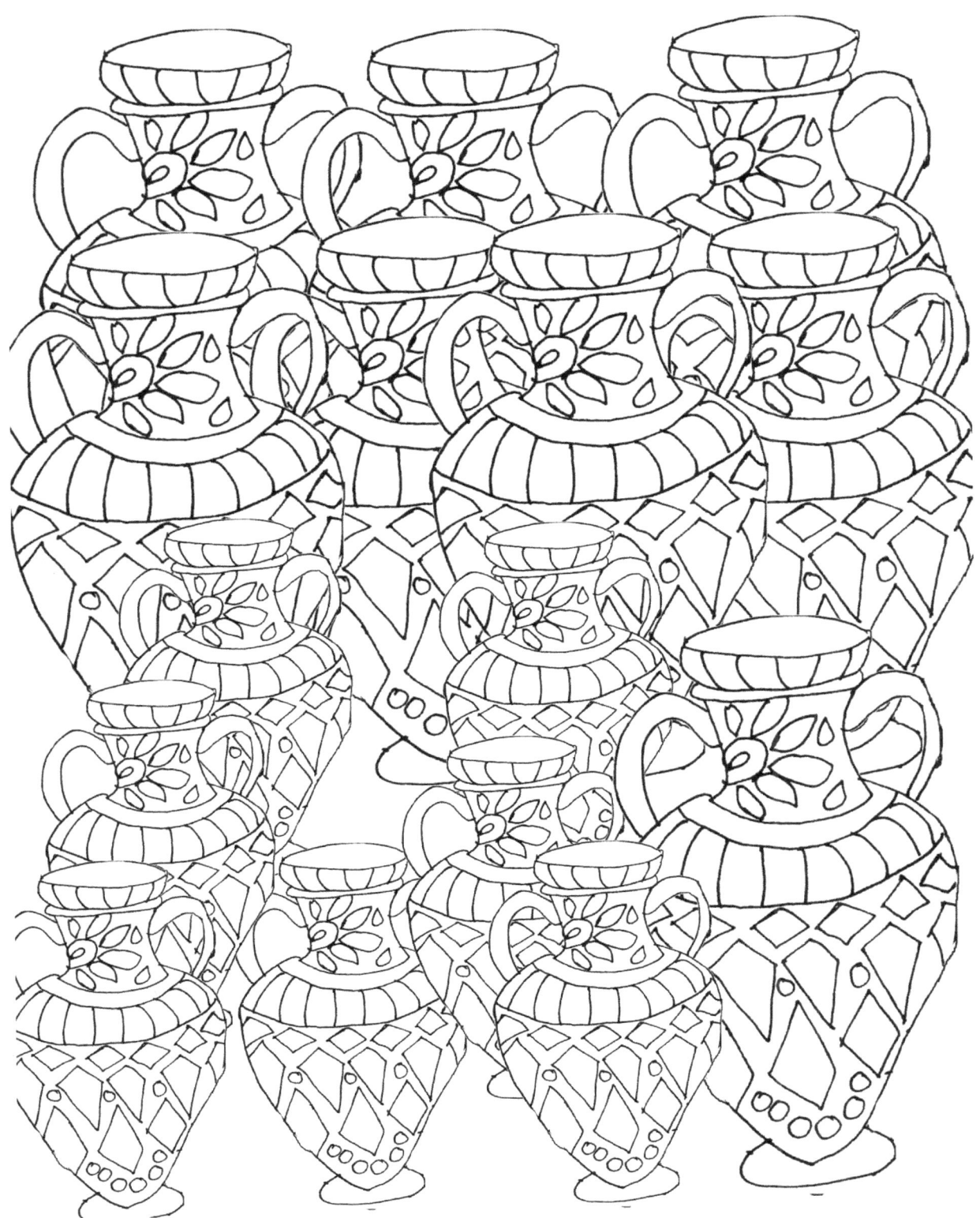

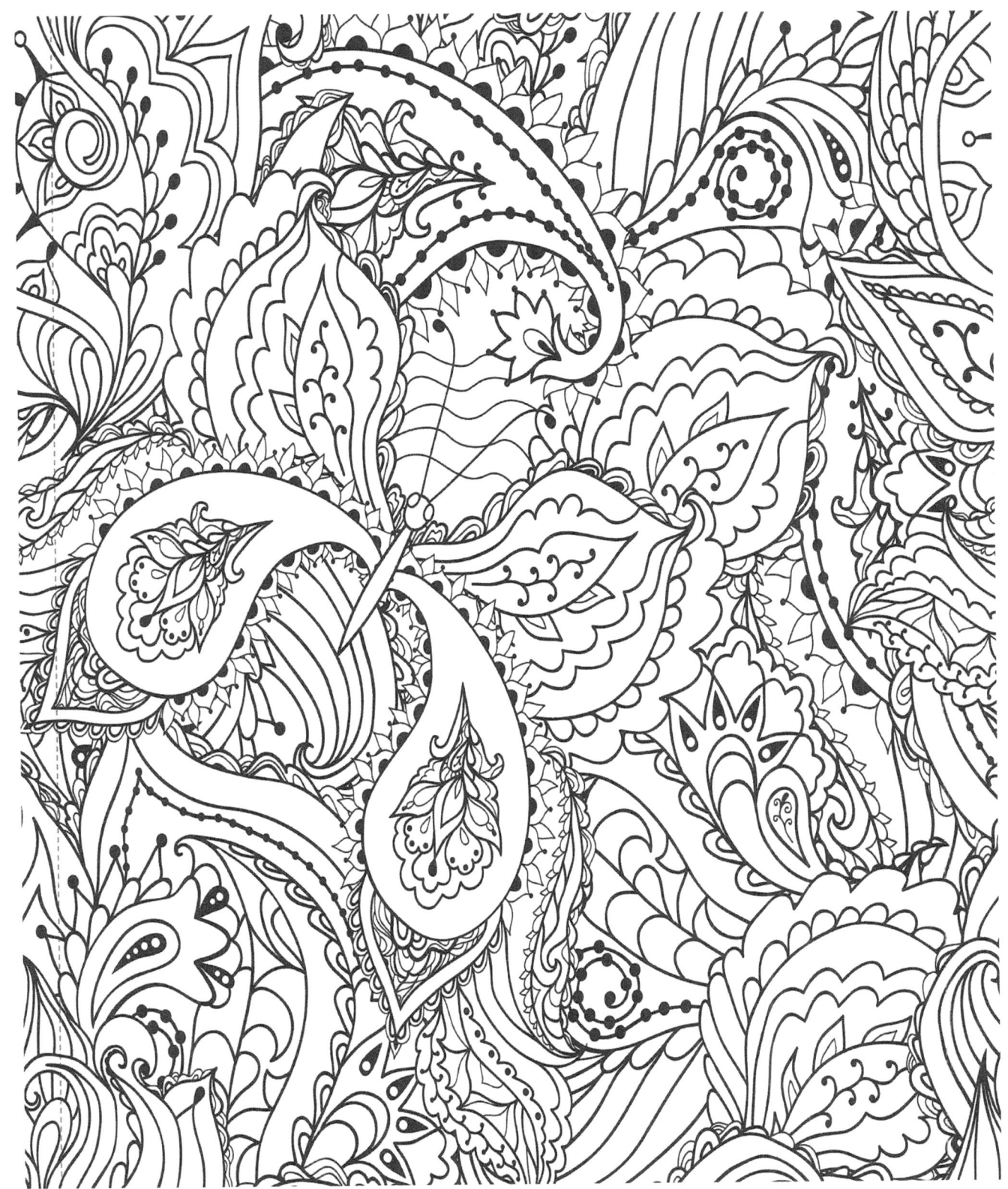

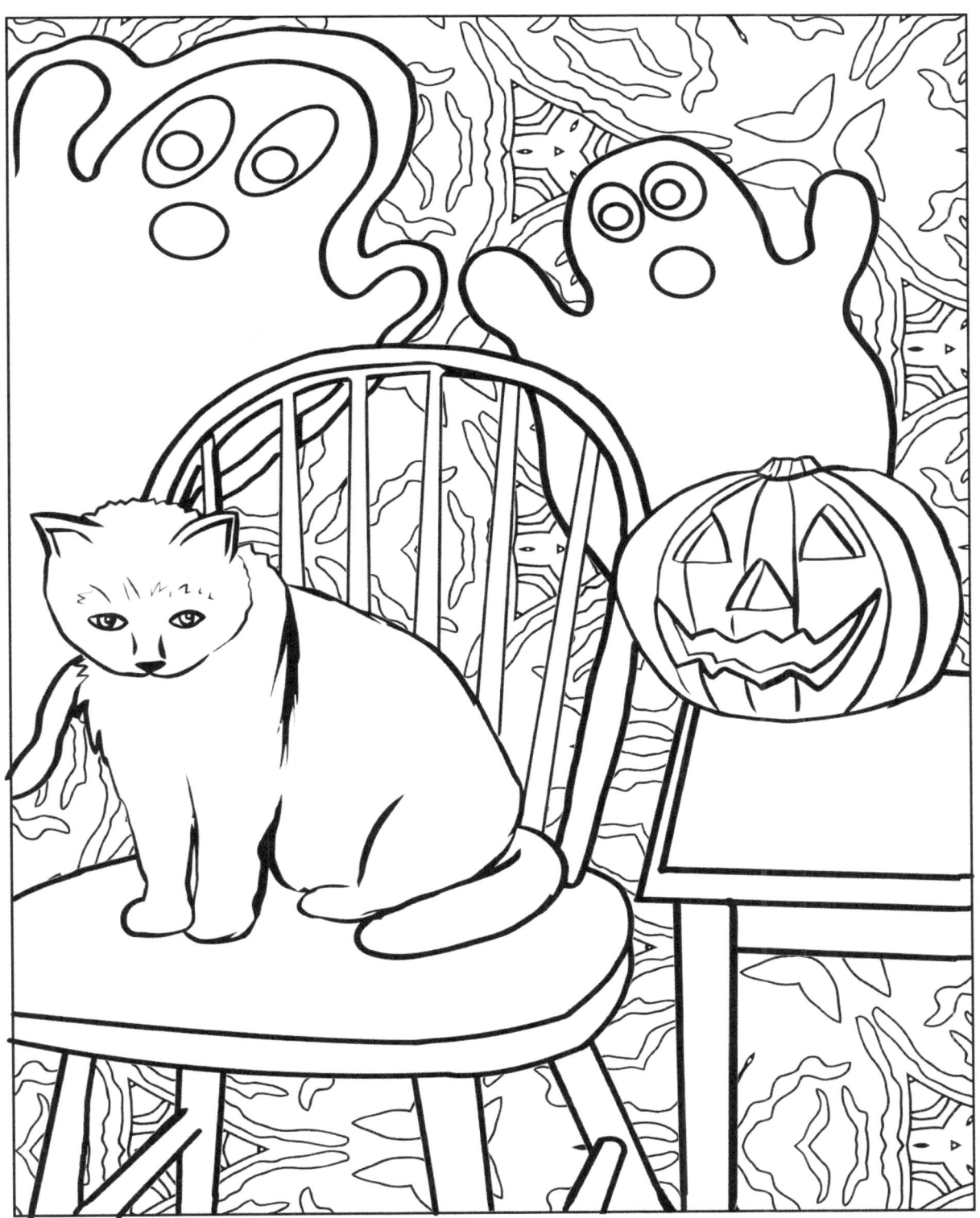

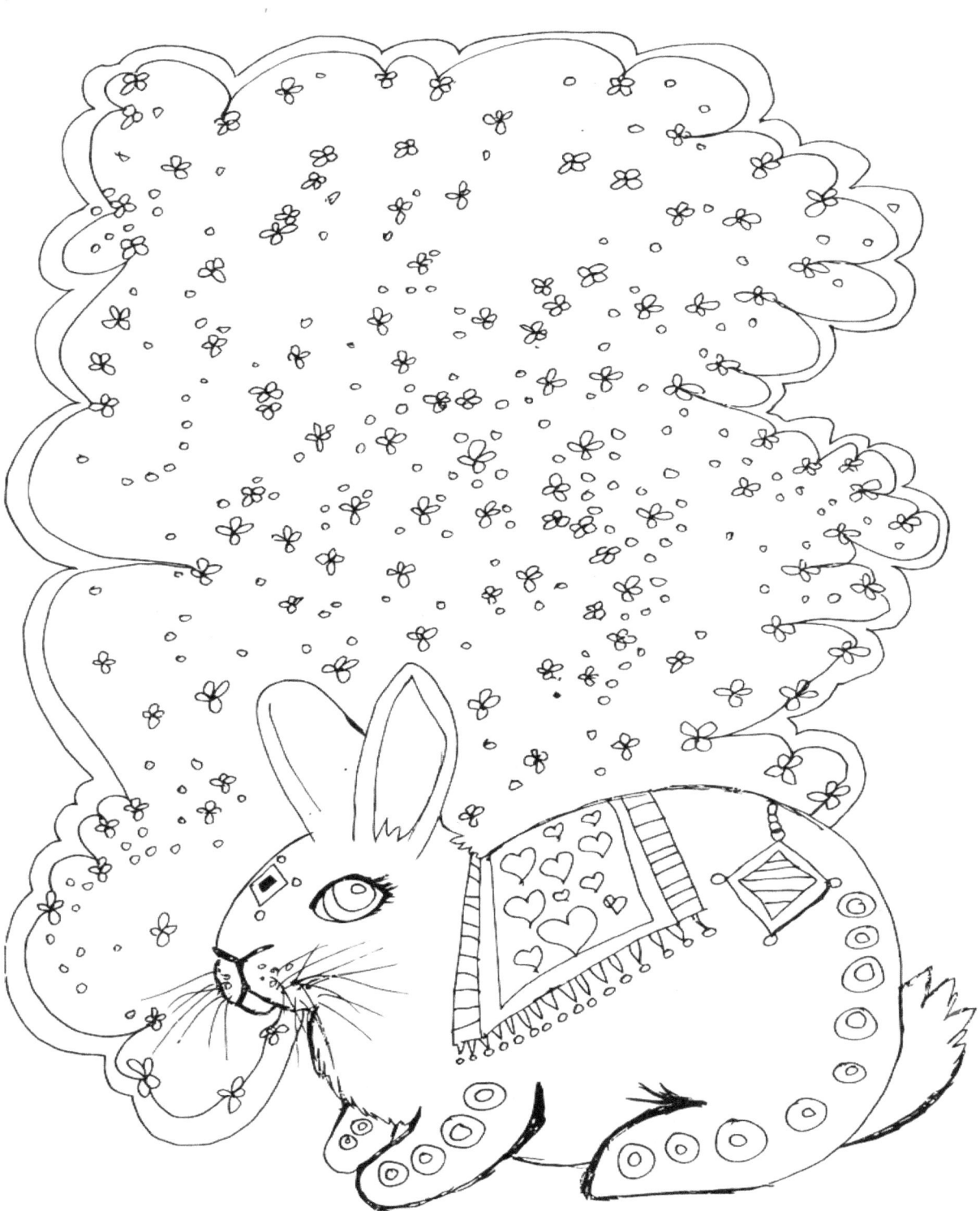

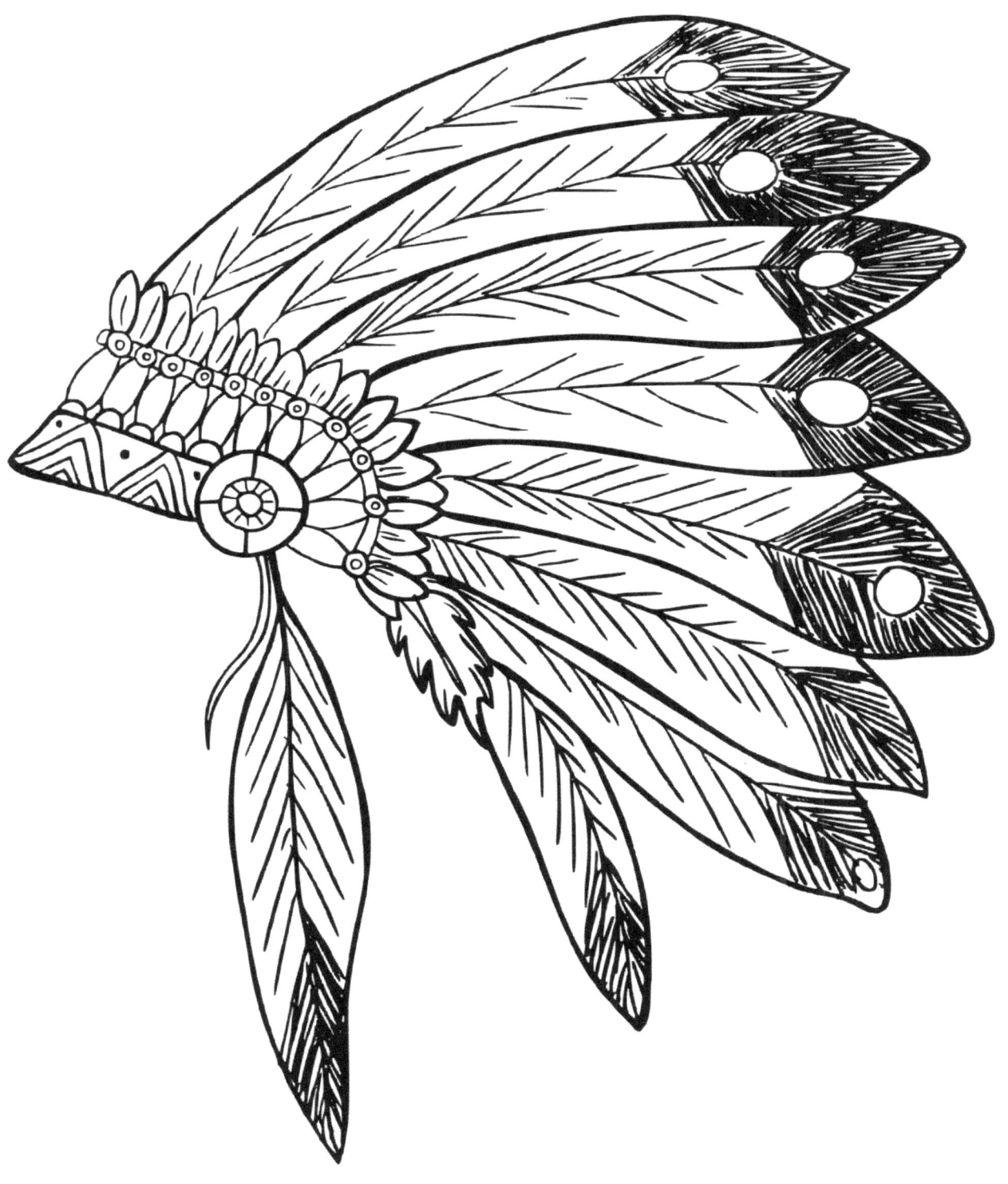

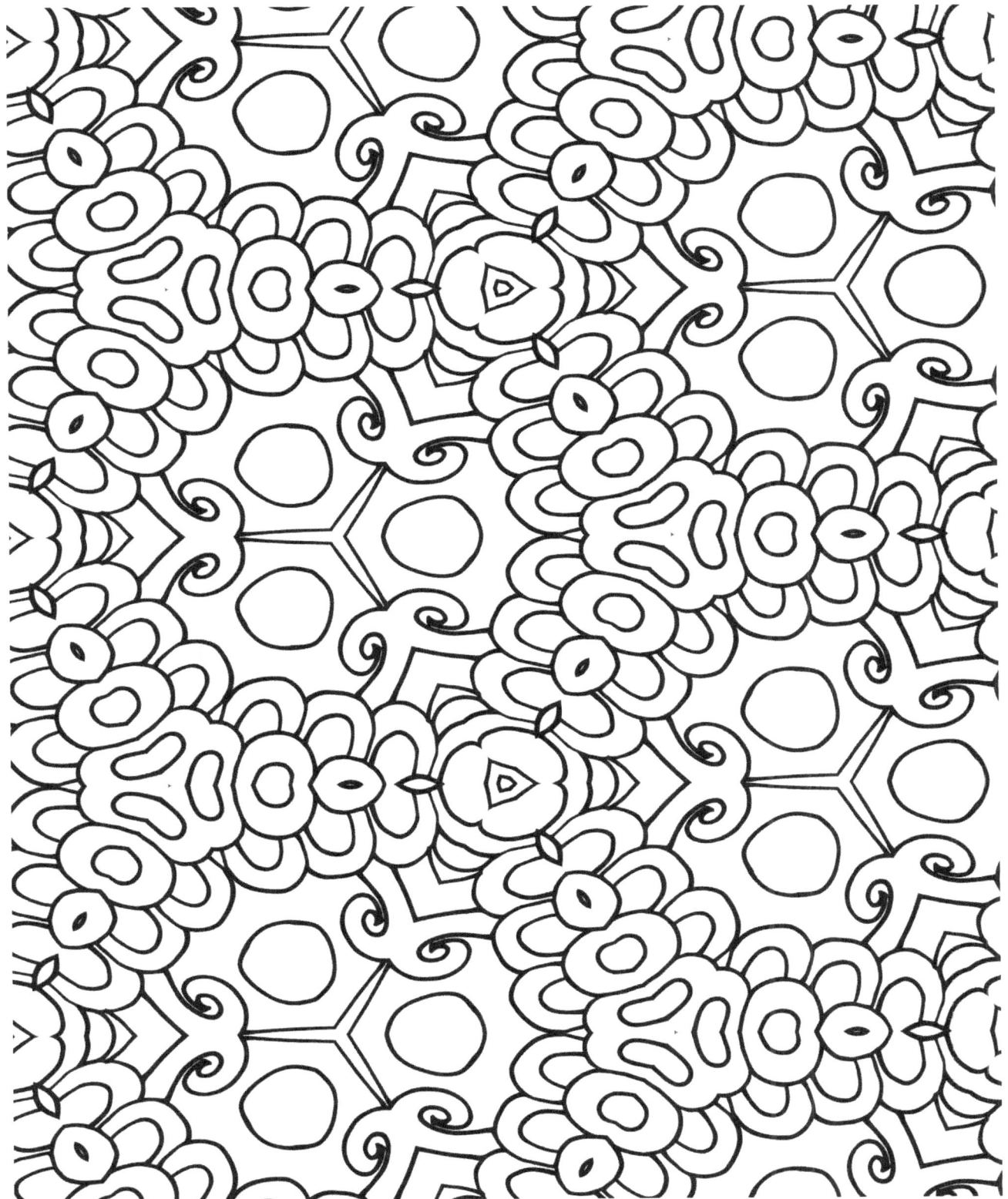

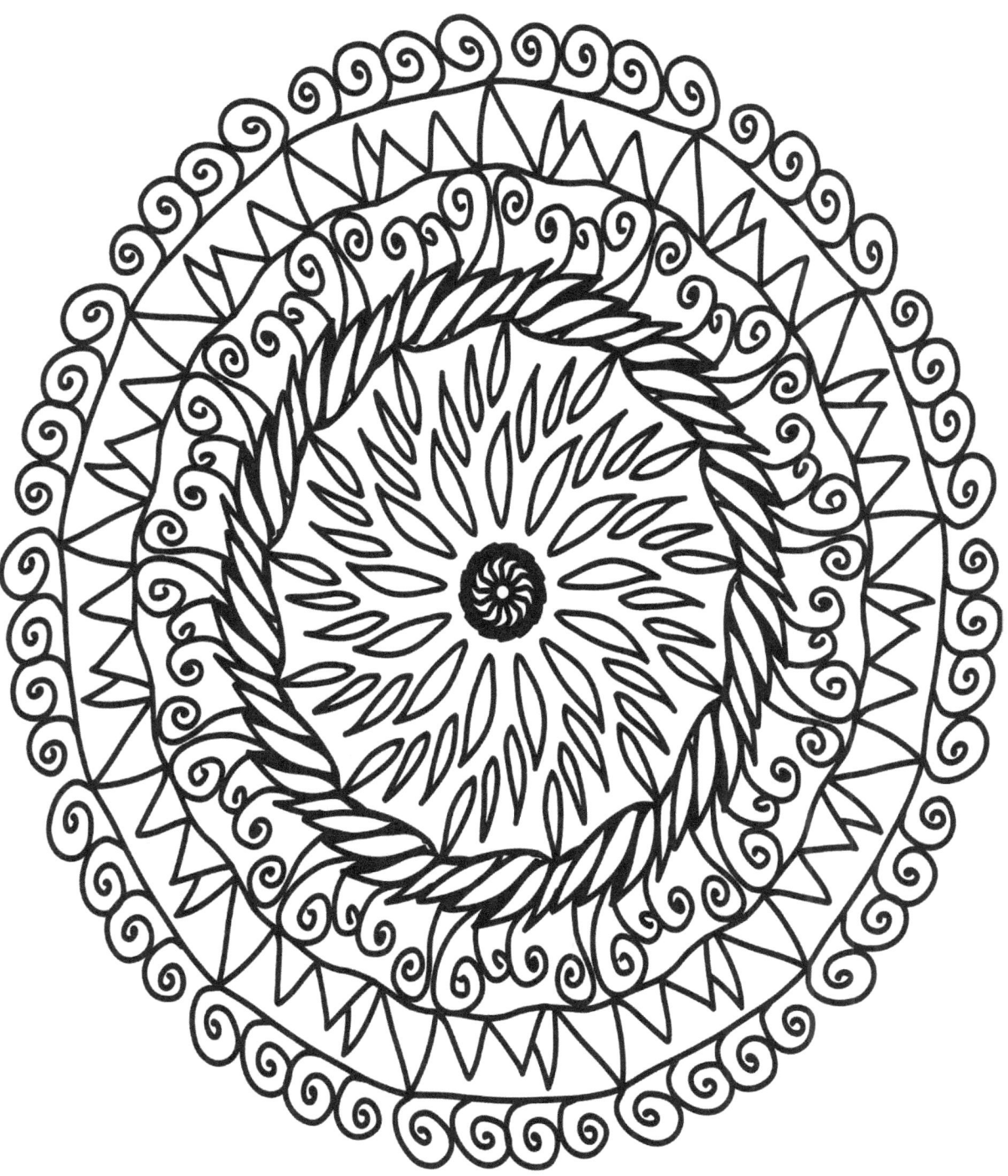

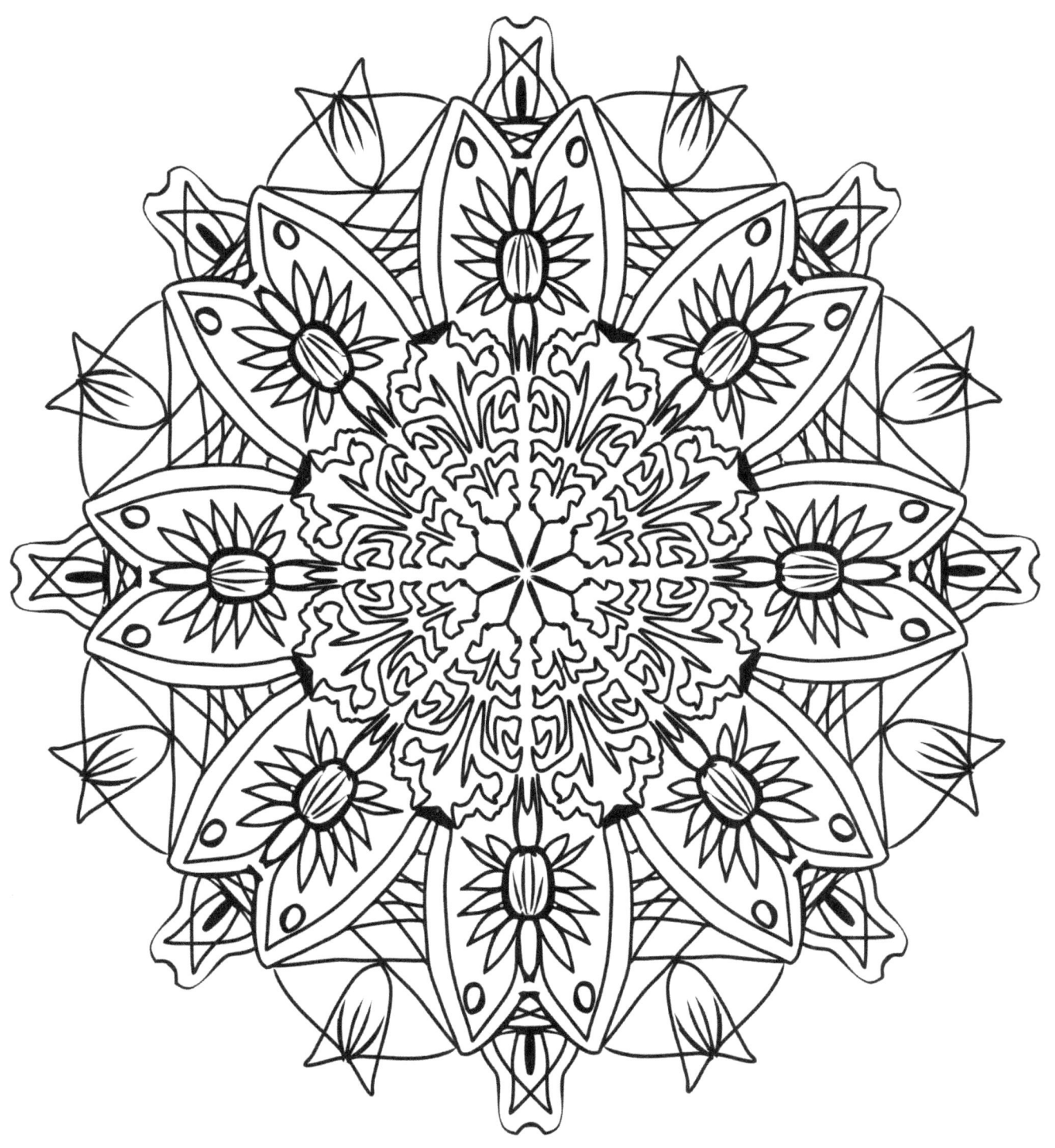

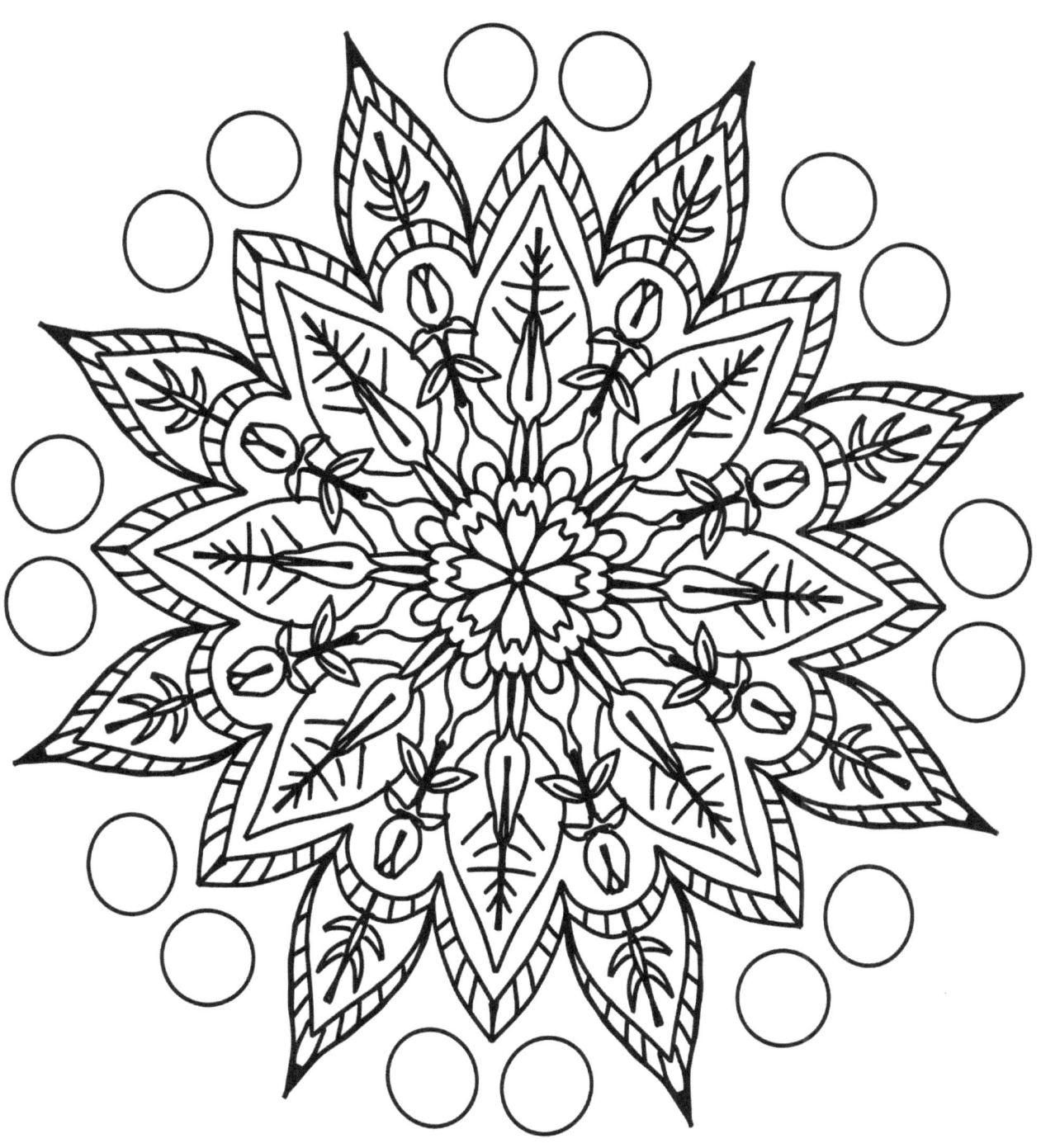

Organized Chaos

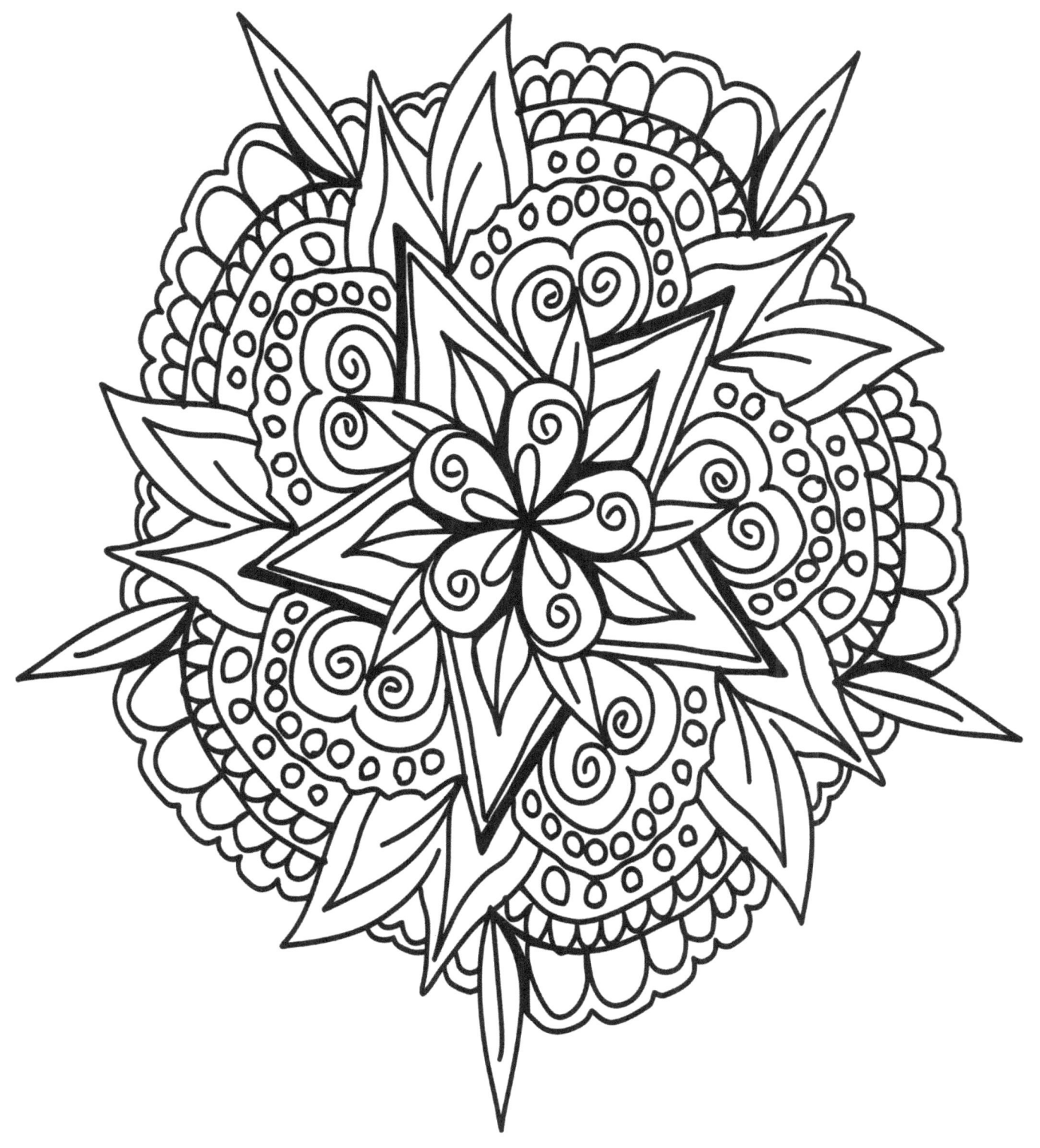

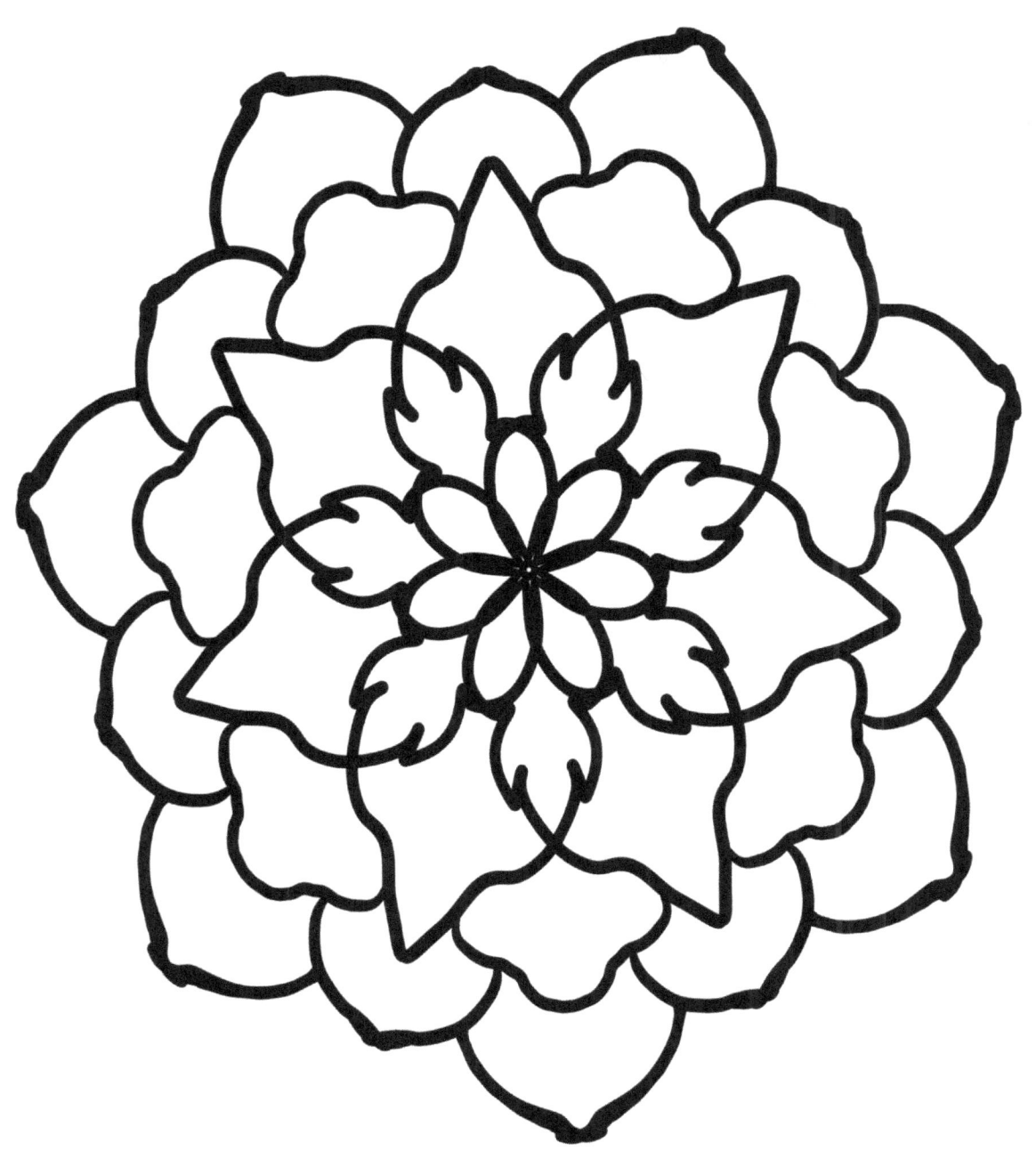

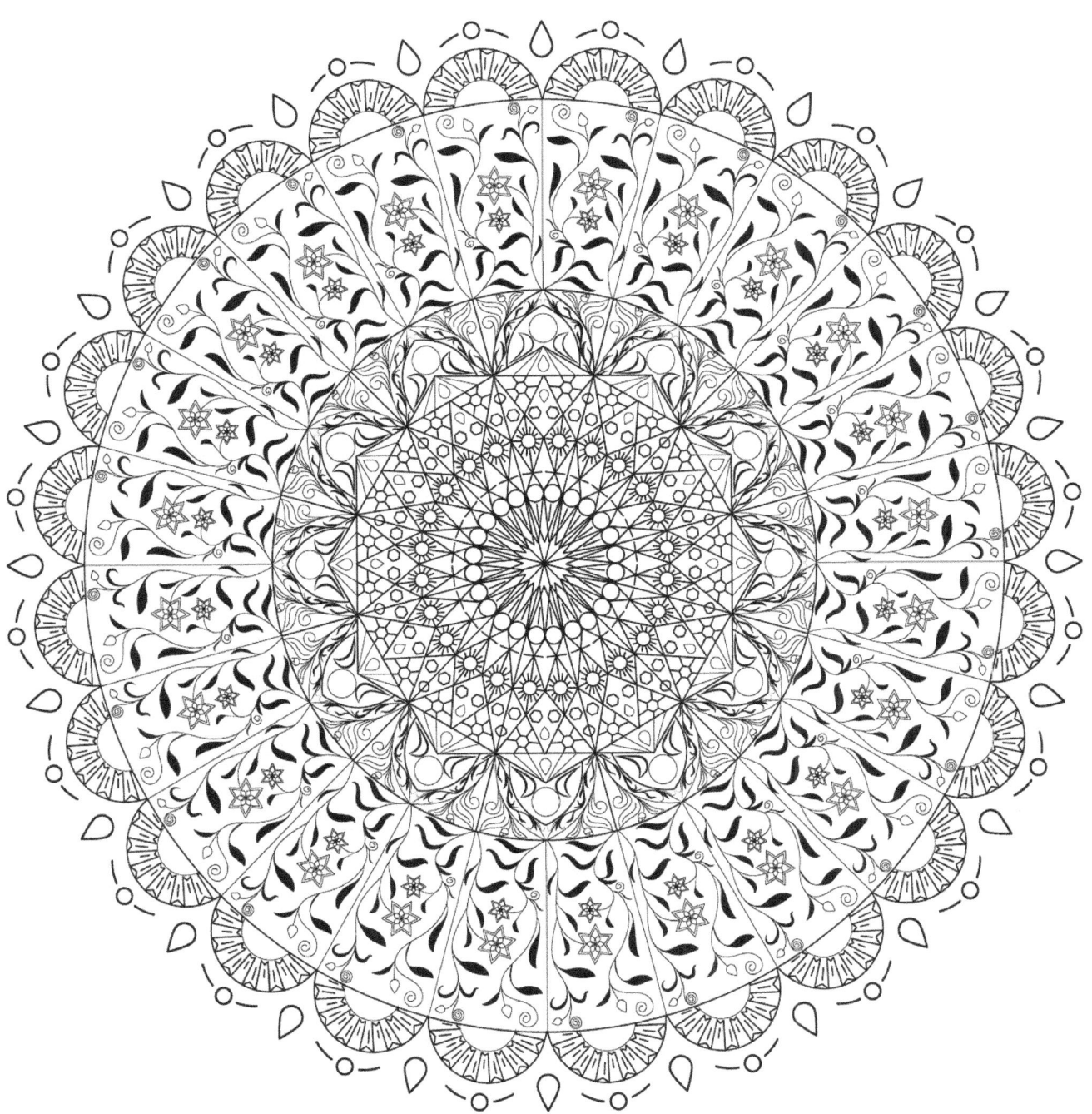

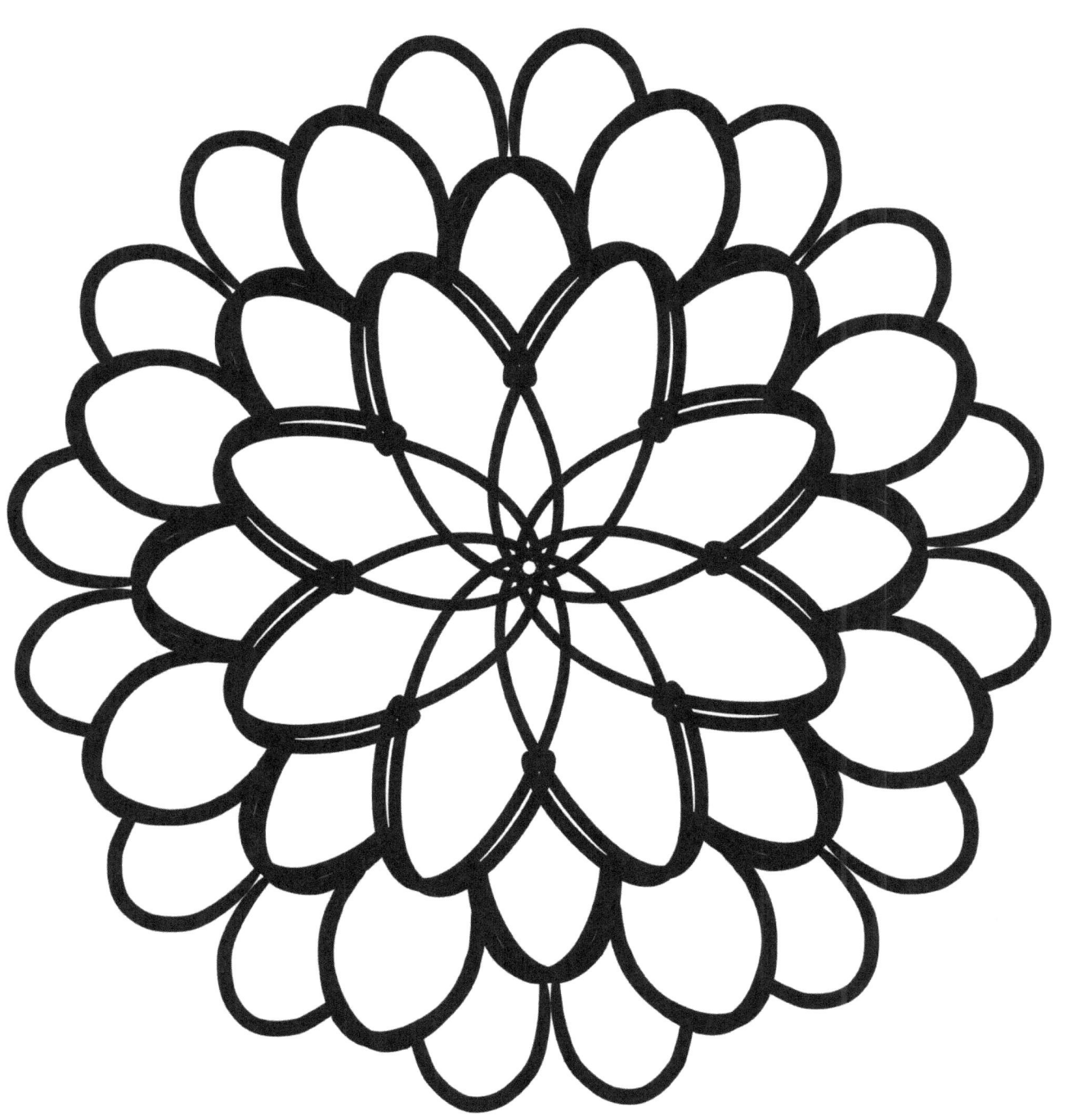

Organized Chaos

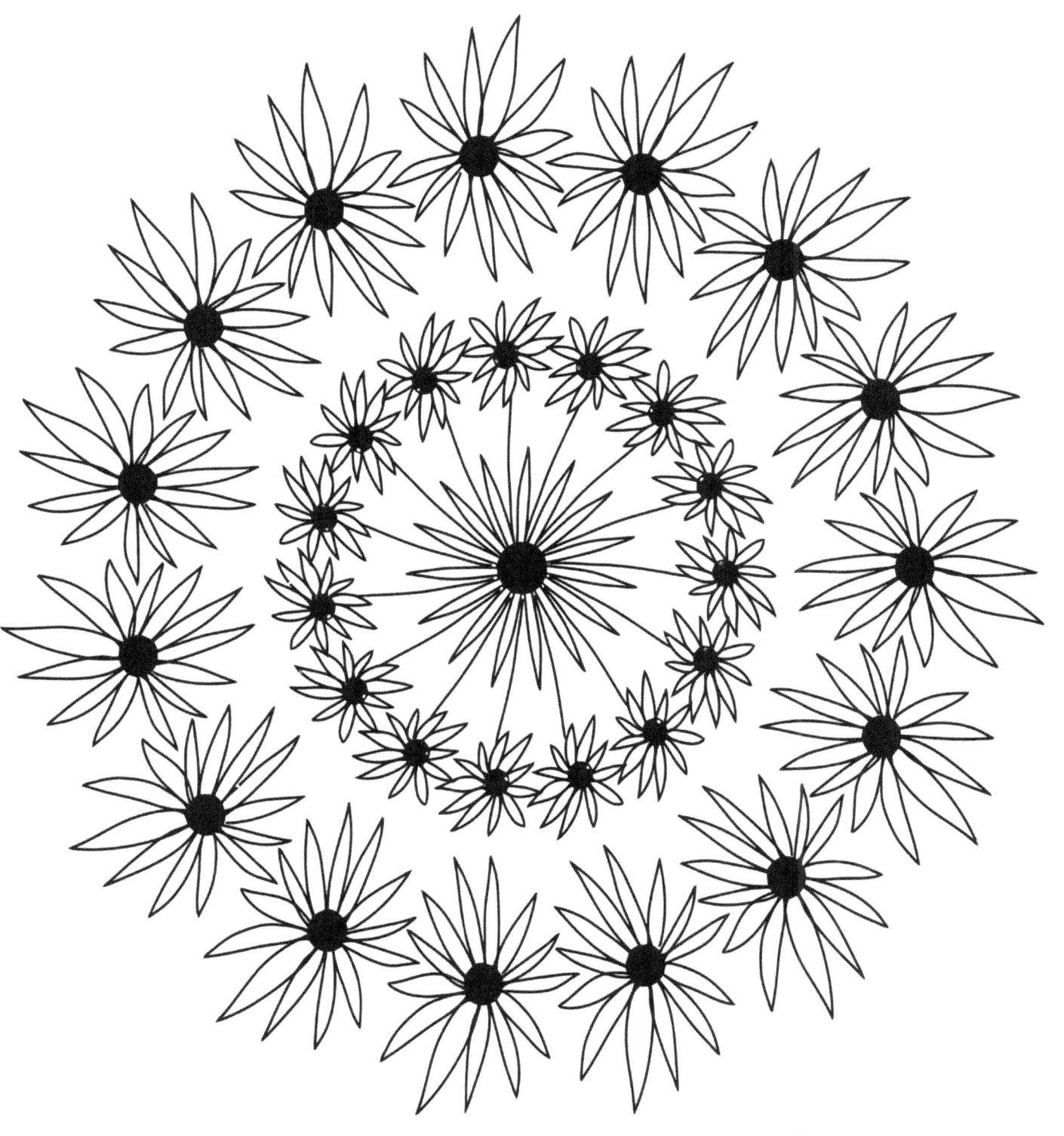

Organized Chaos

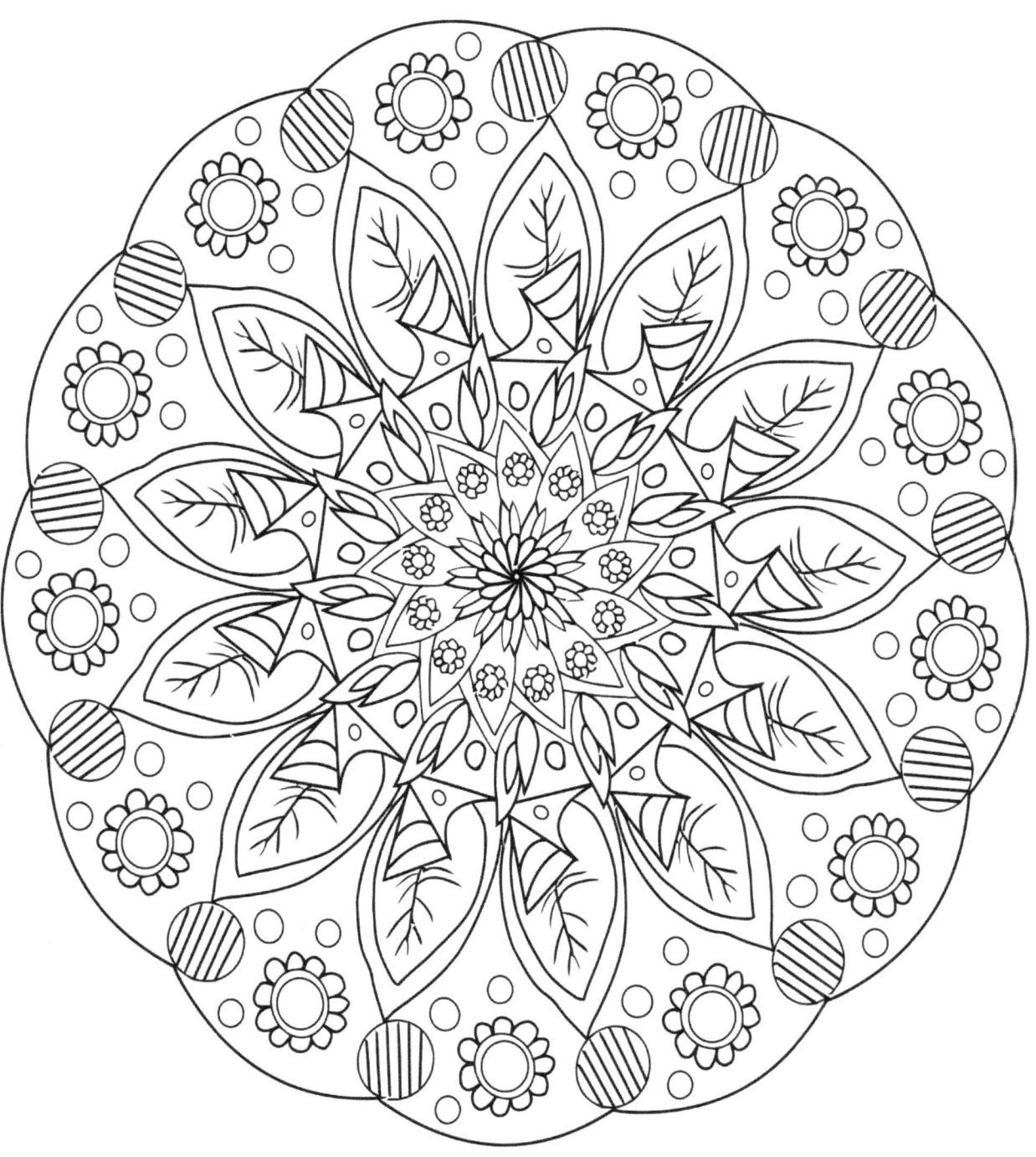

Organized Chaos

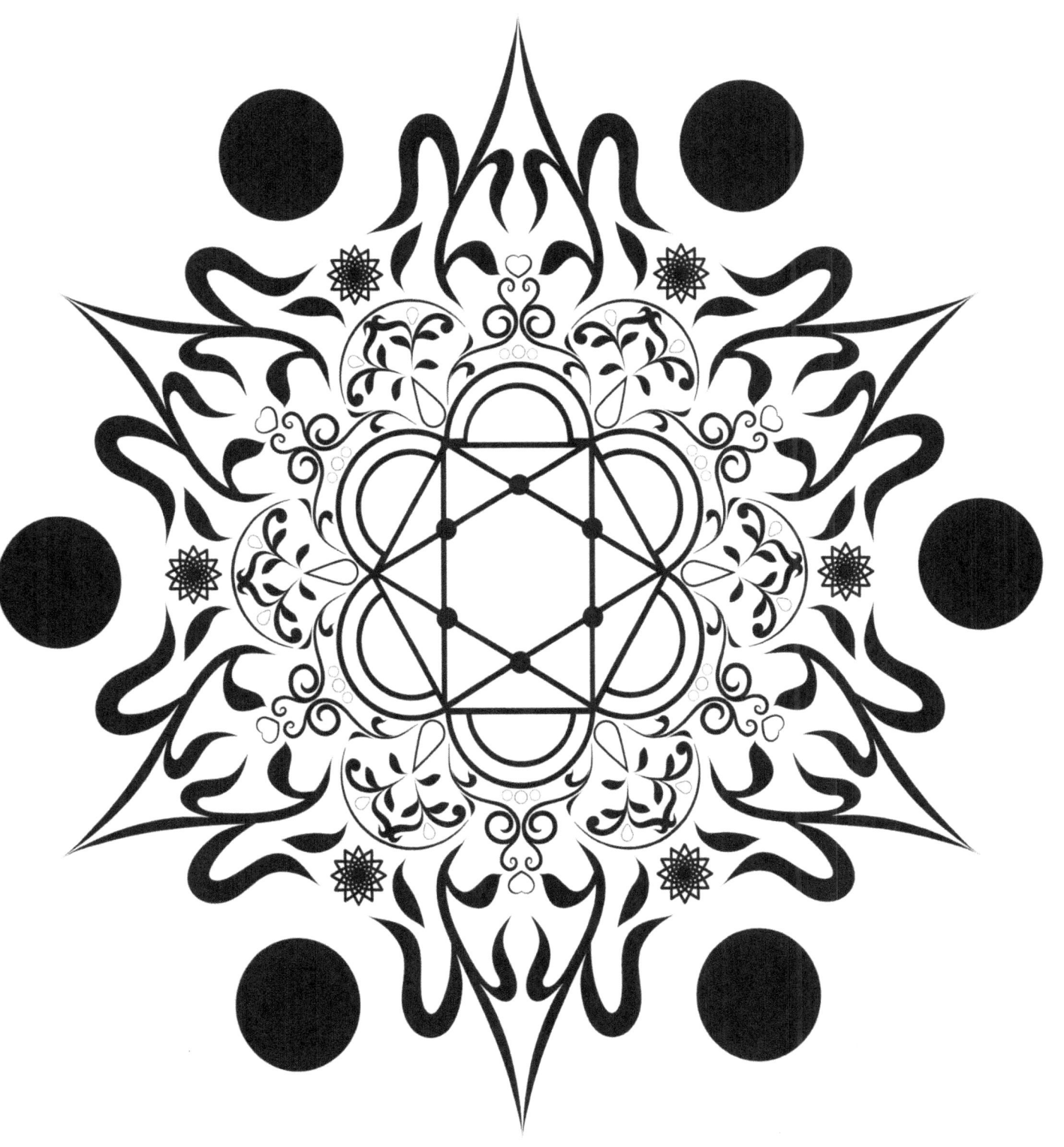

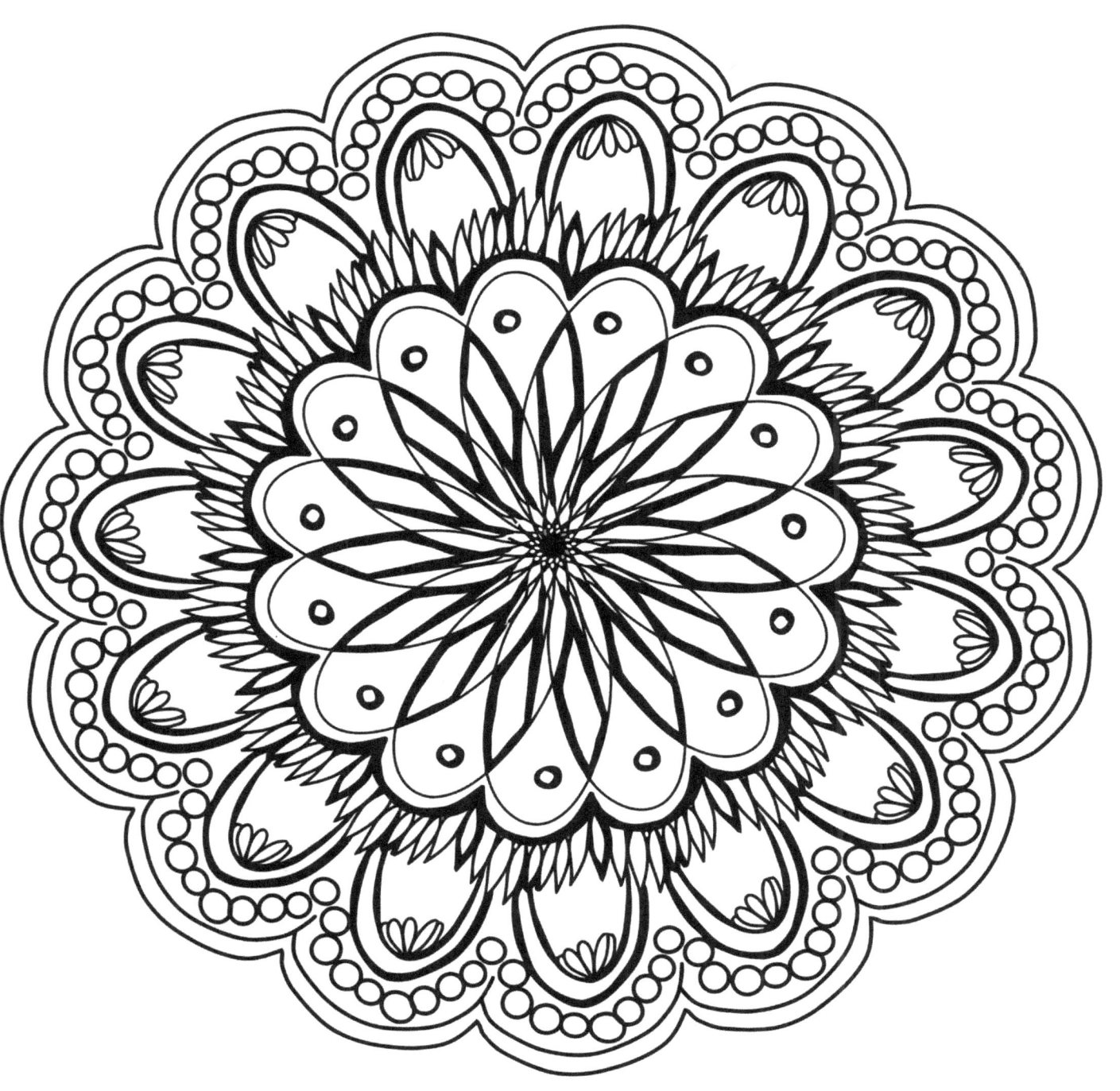

Organized Chaos

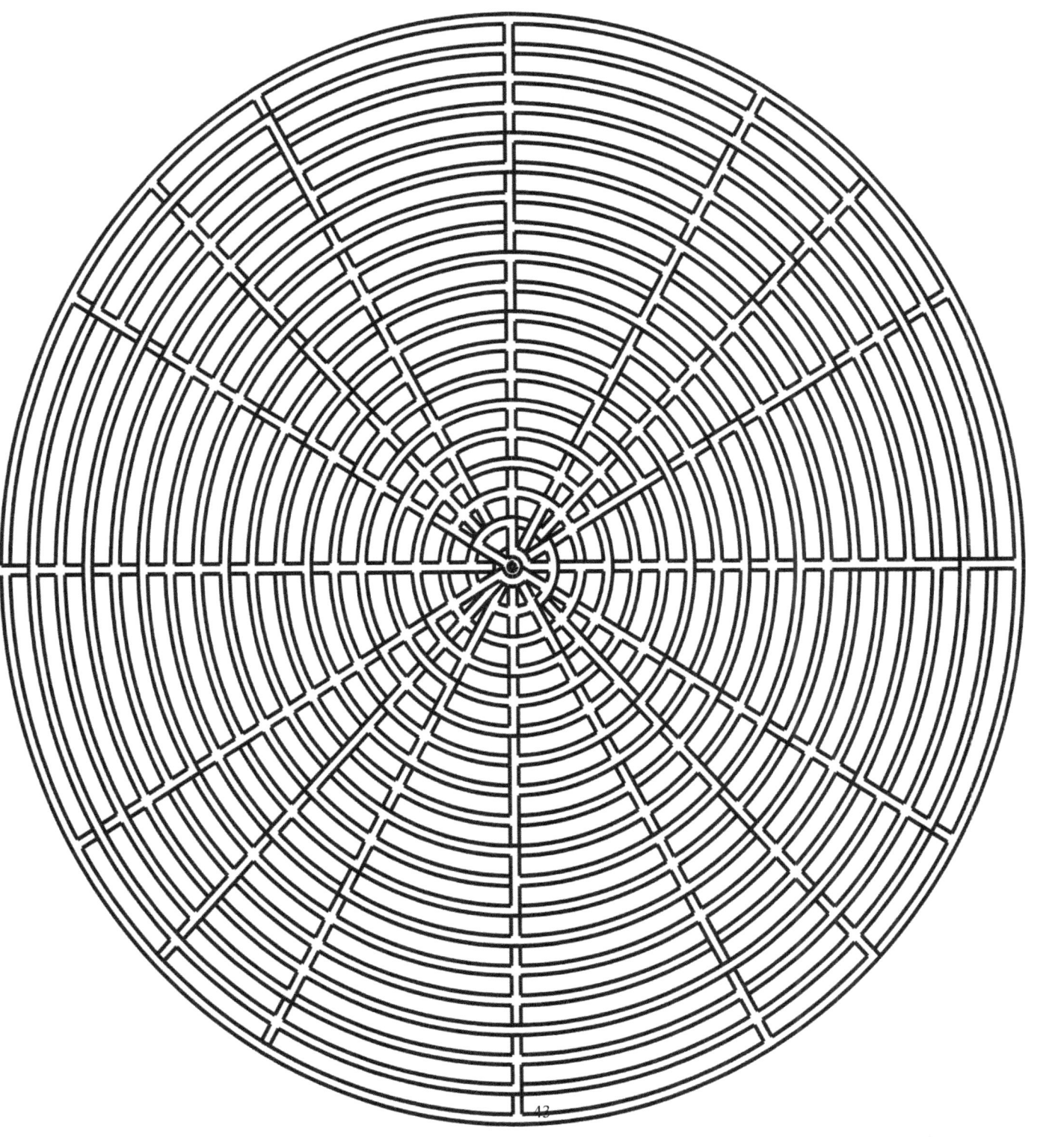

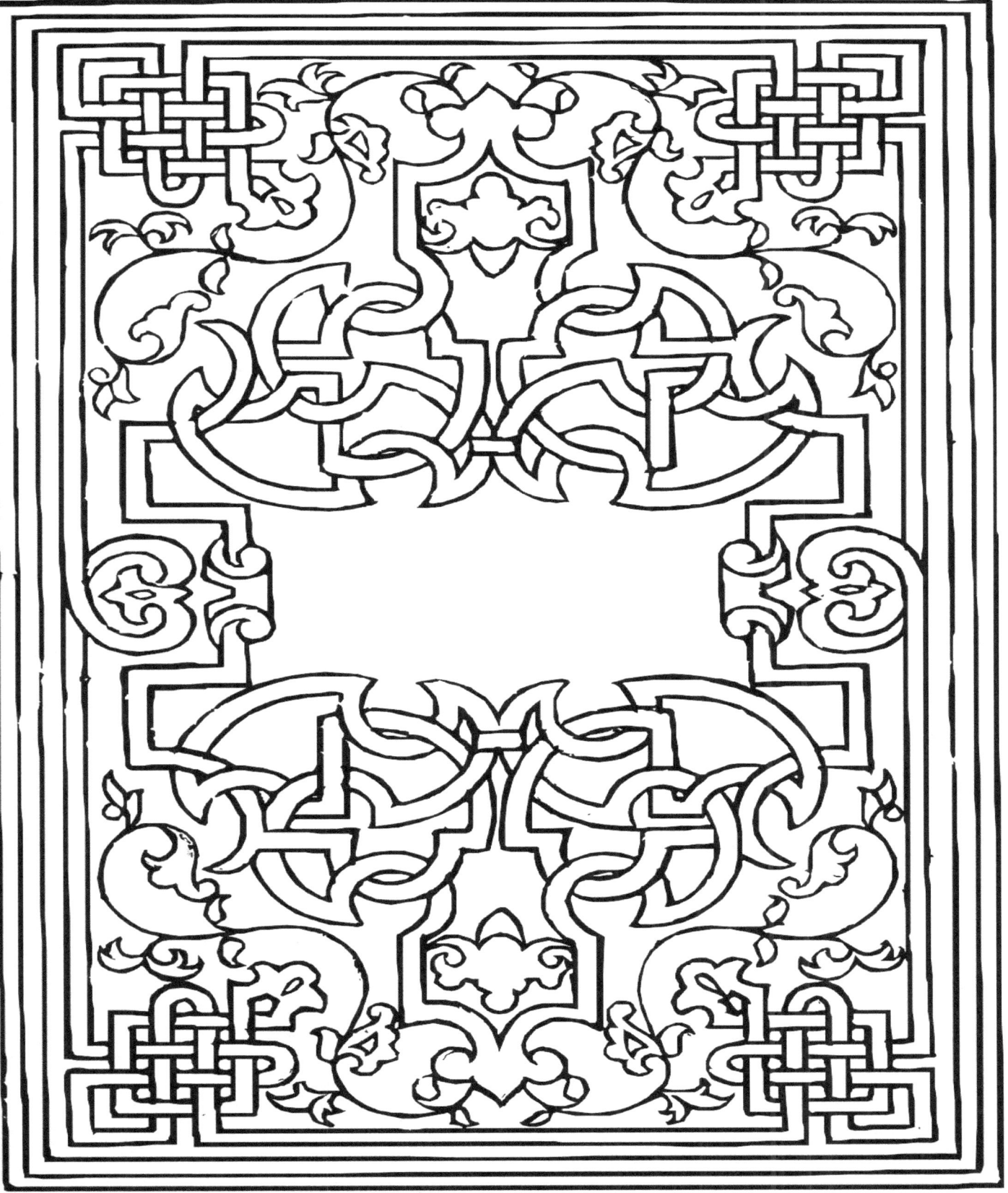

Organized Chaos

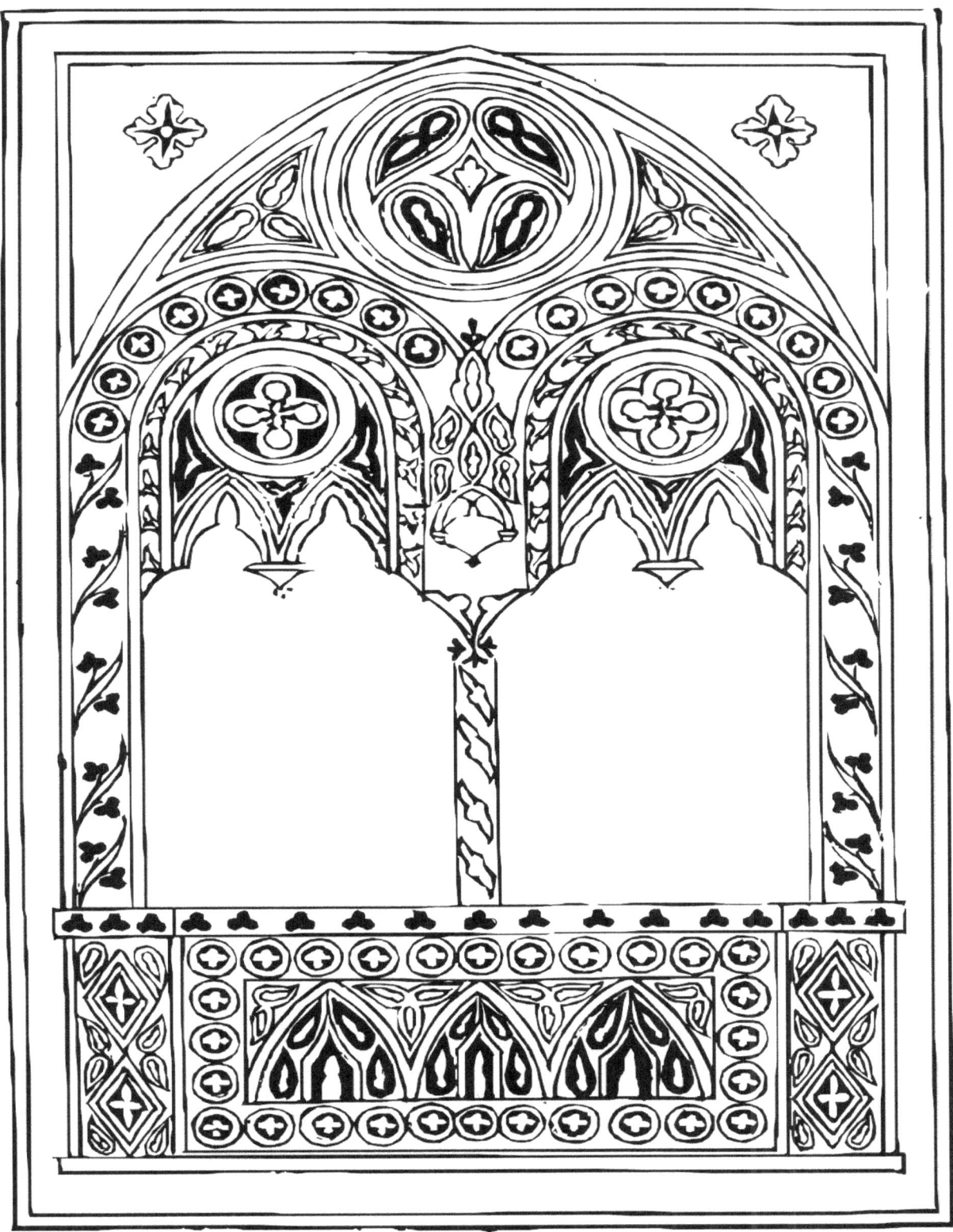

Organized Chaos

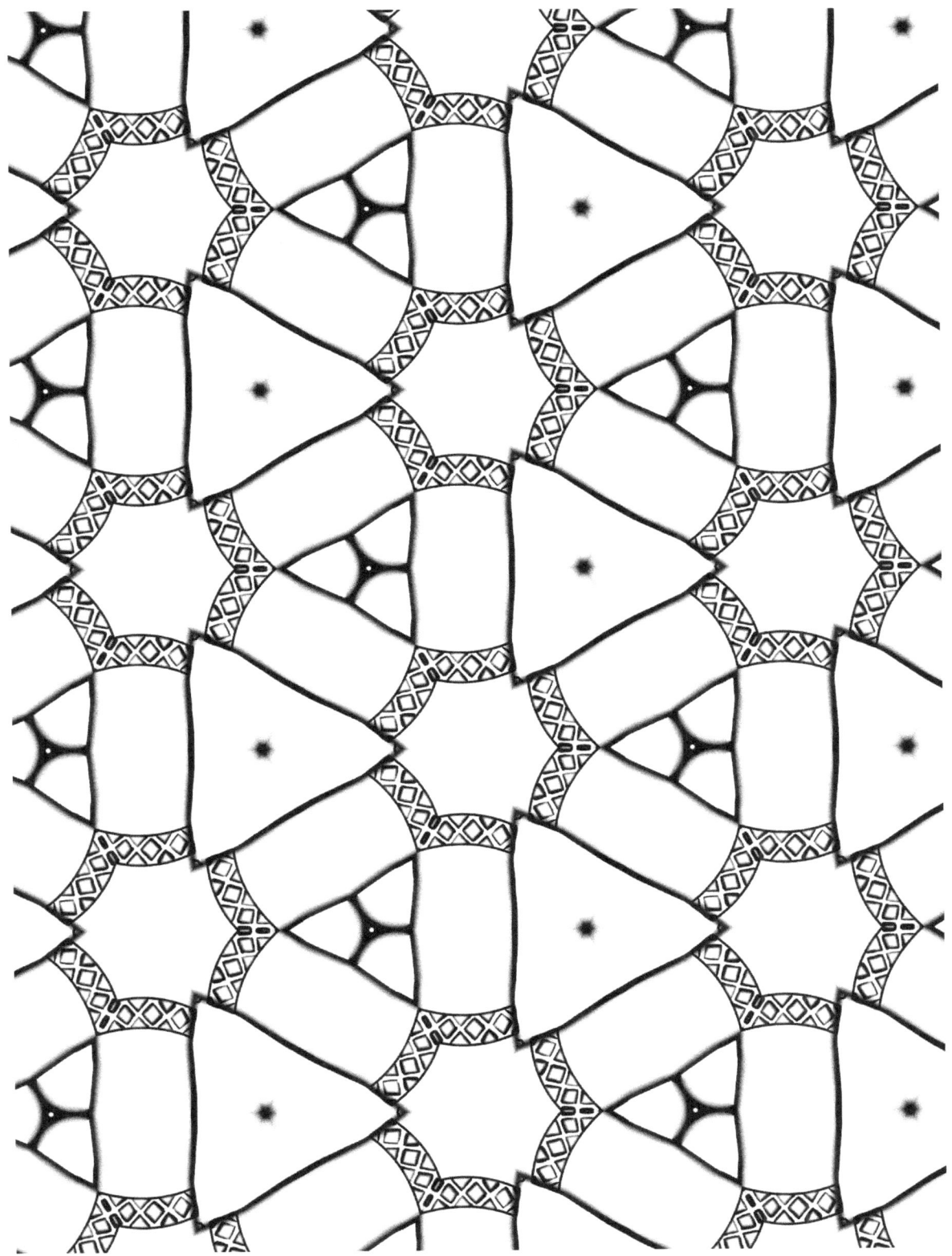

Organized Chaos

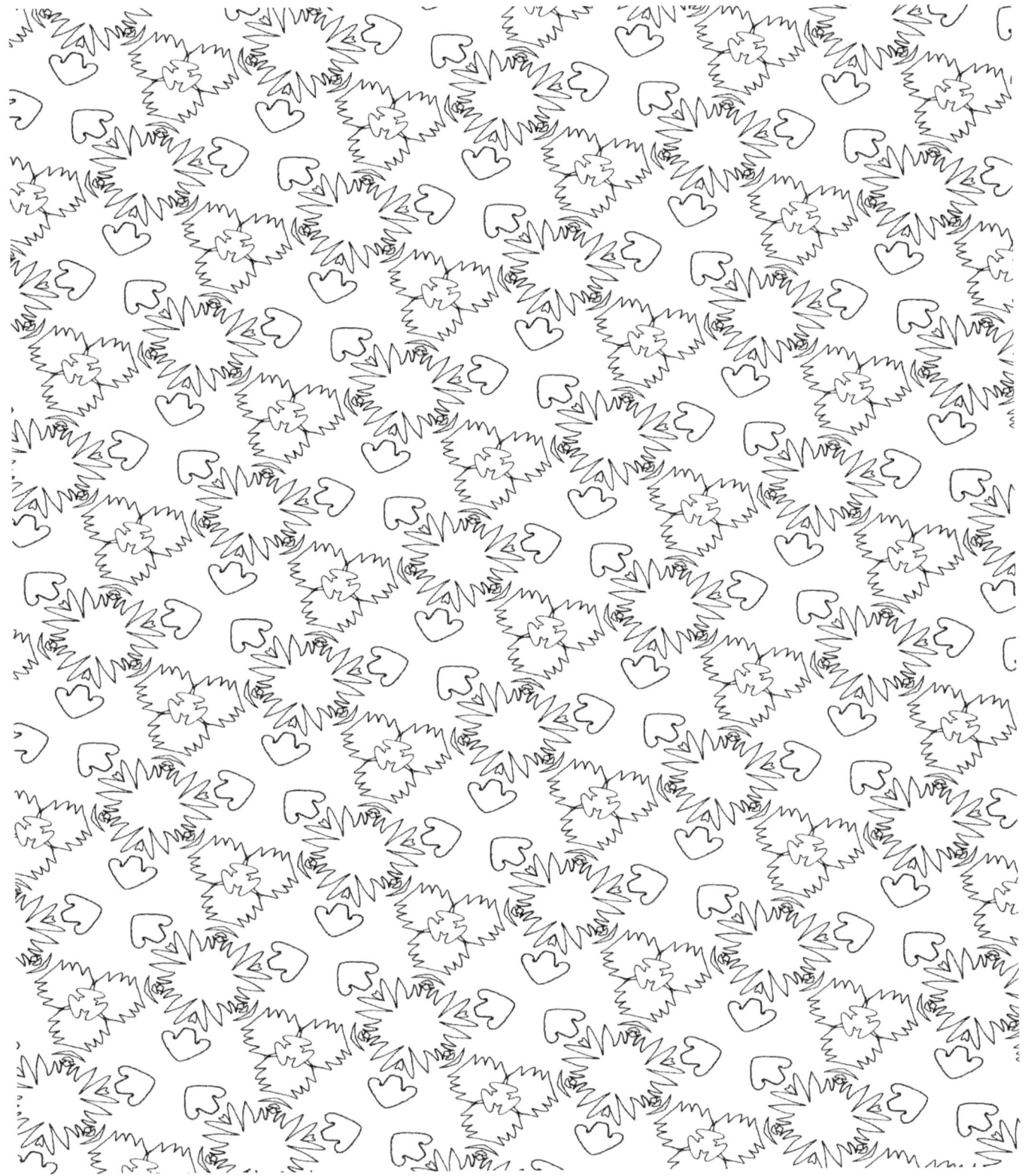

Organized Chaos

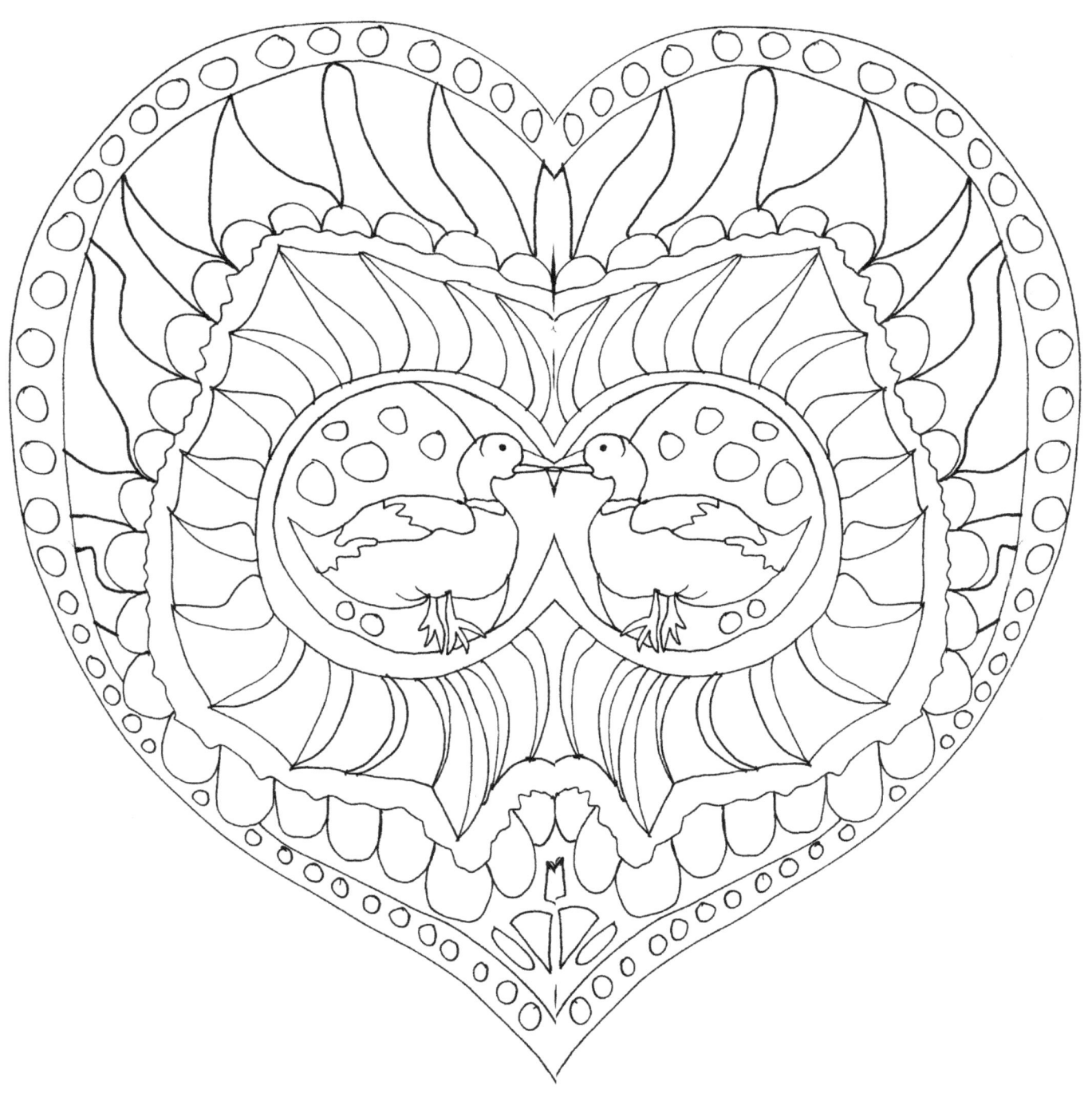

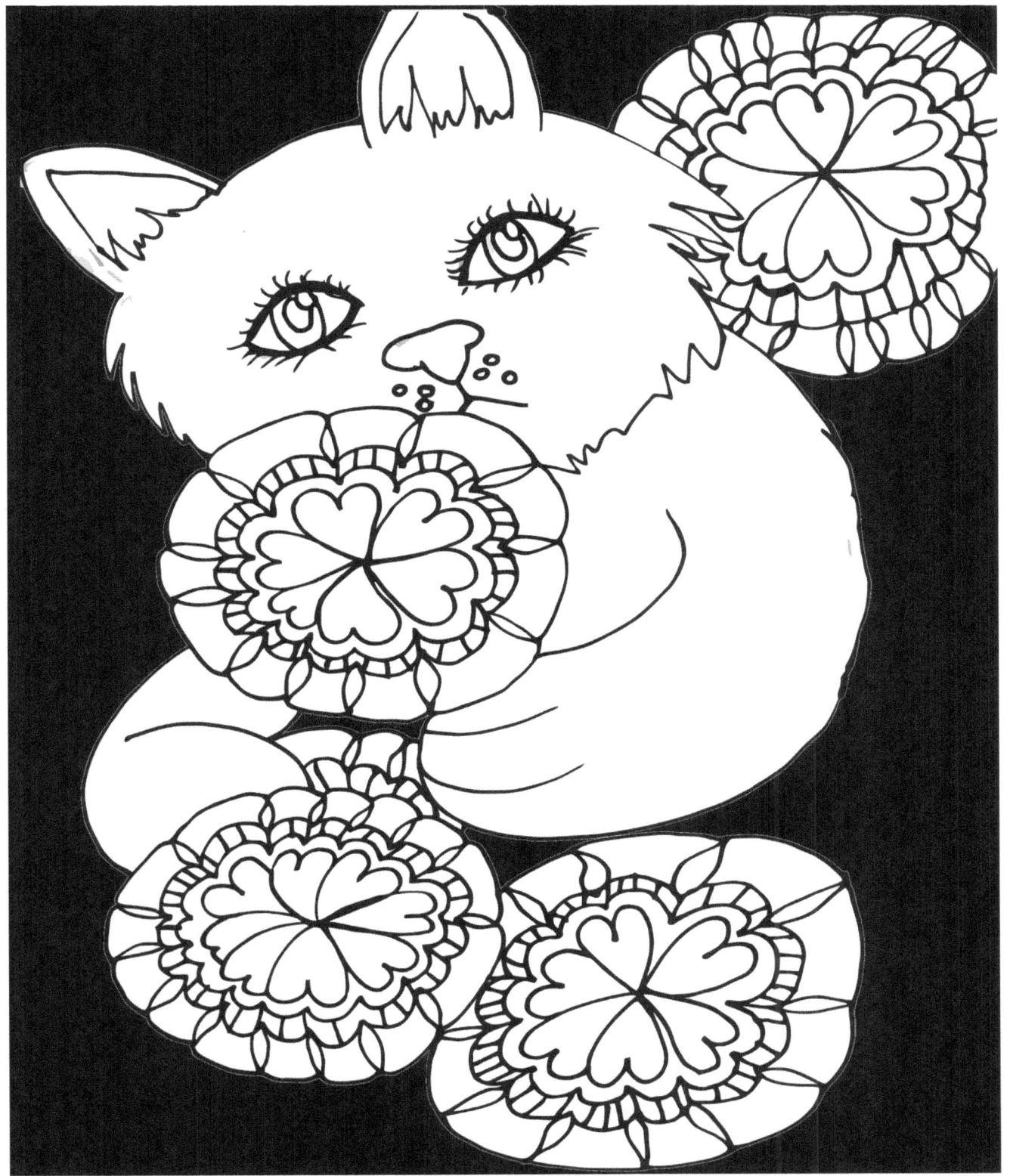

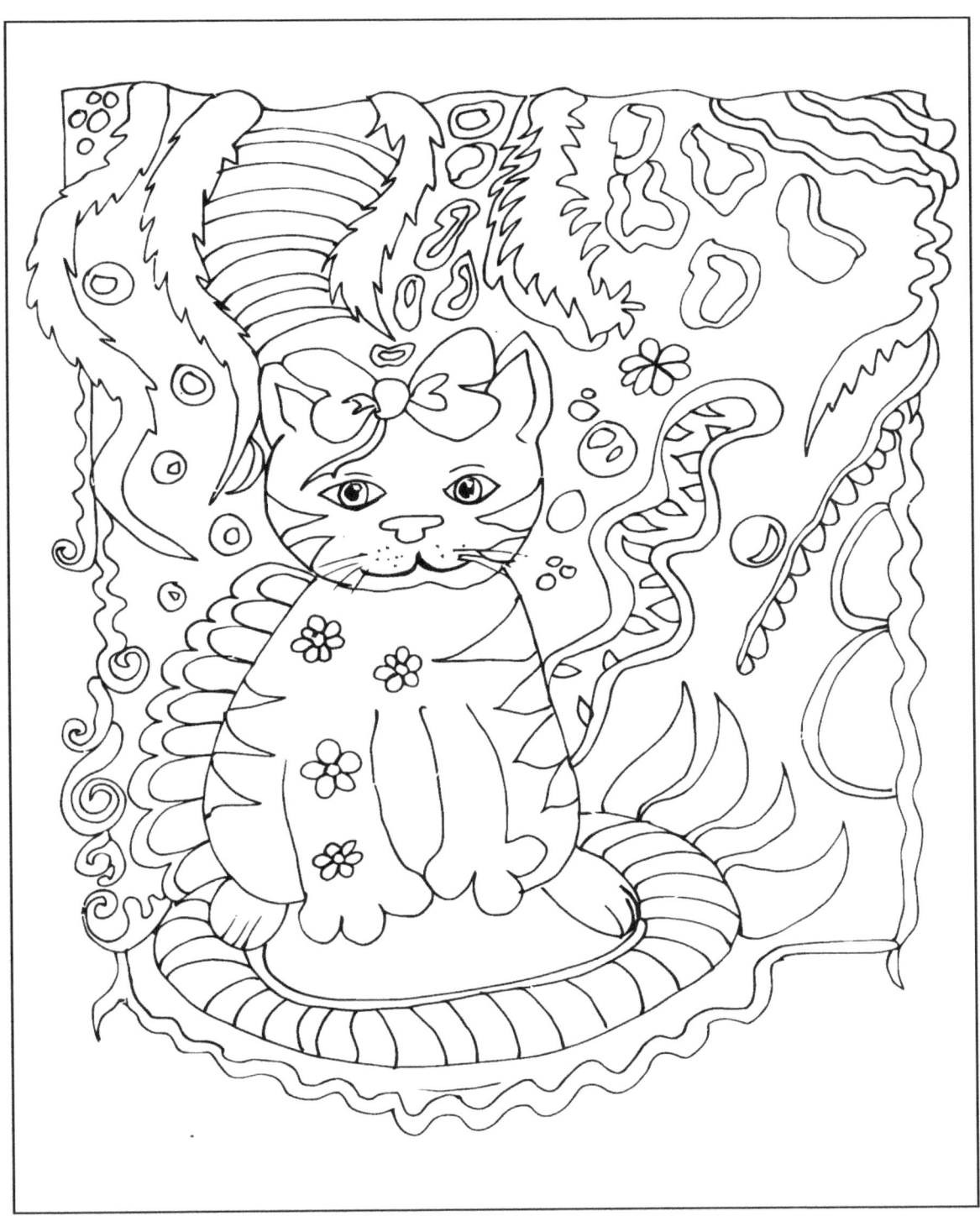

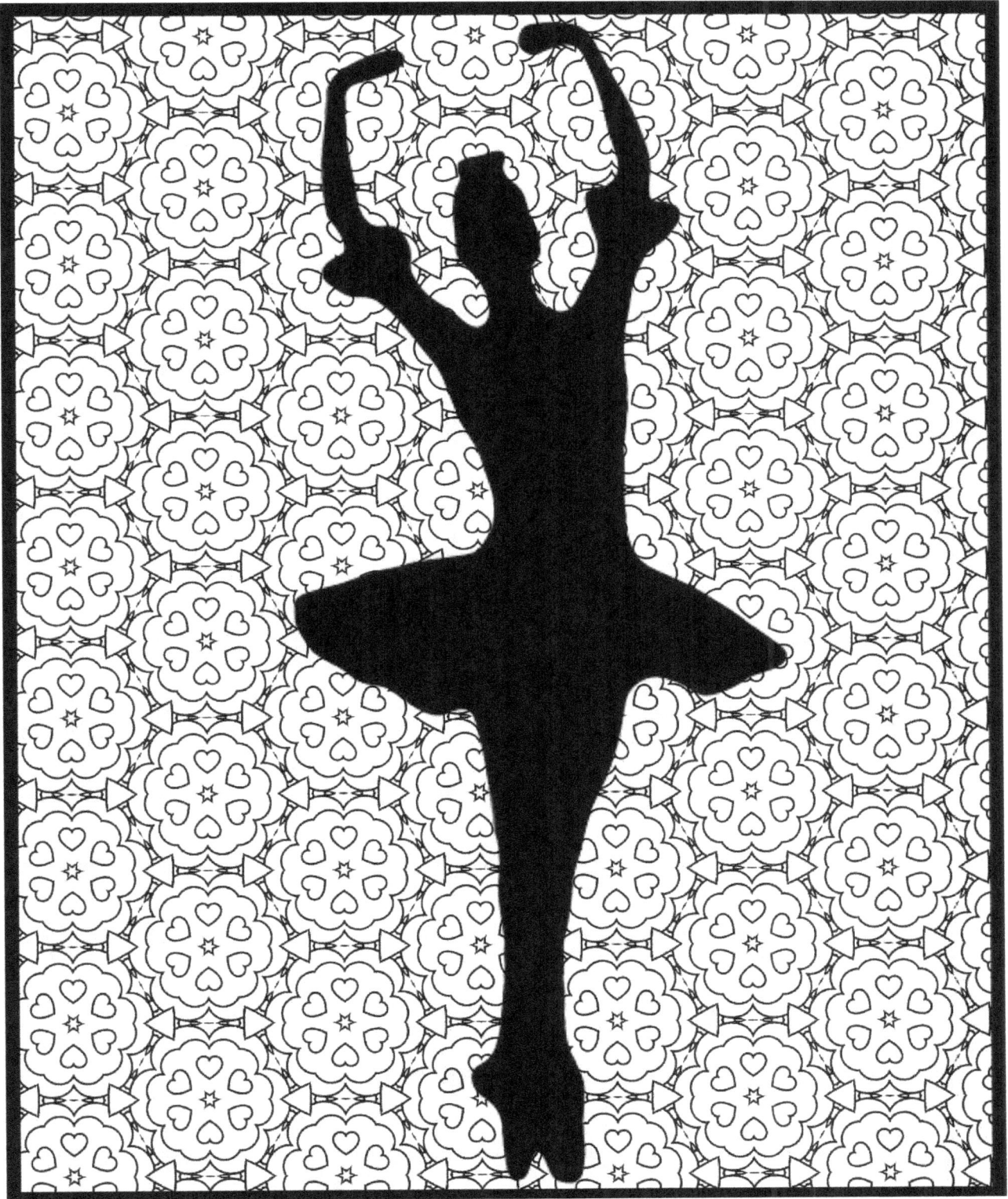

Organized Chaos

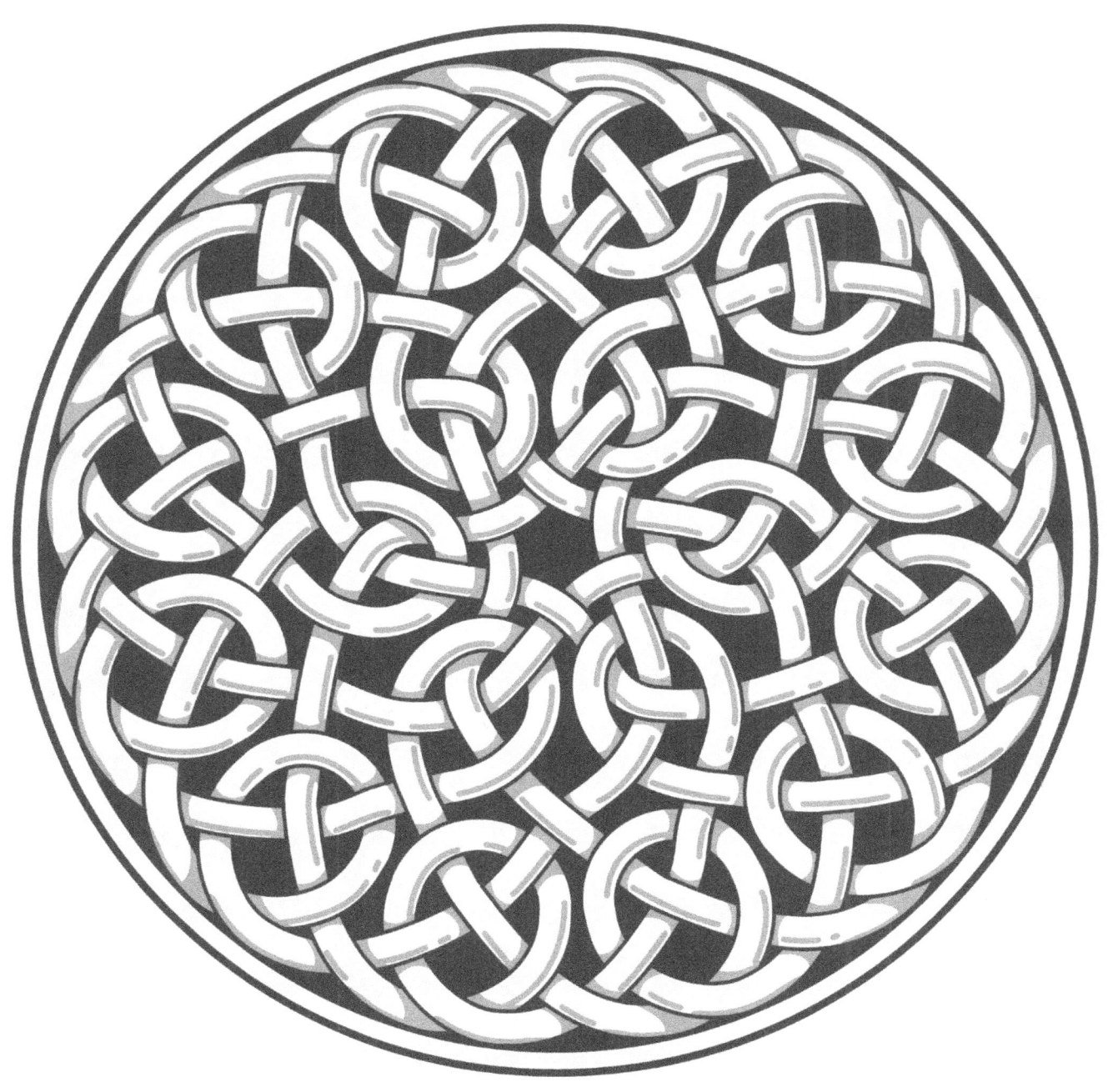

Organized Chaos

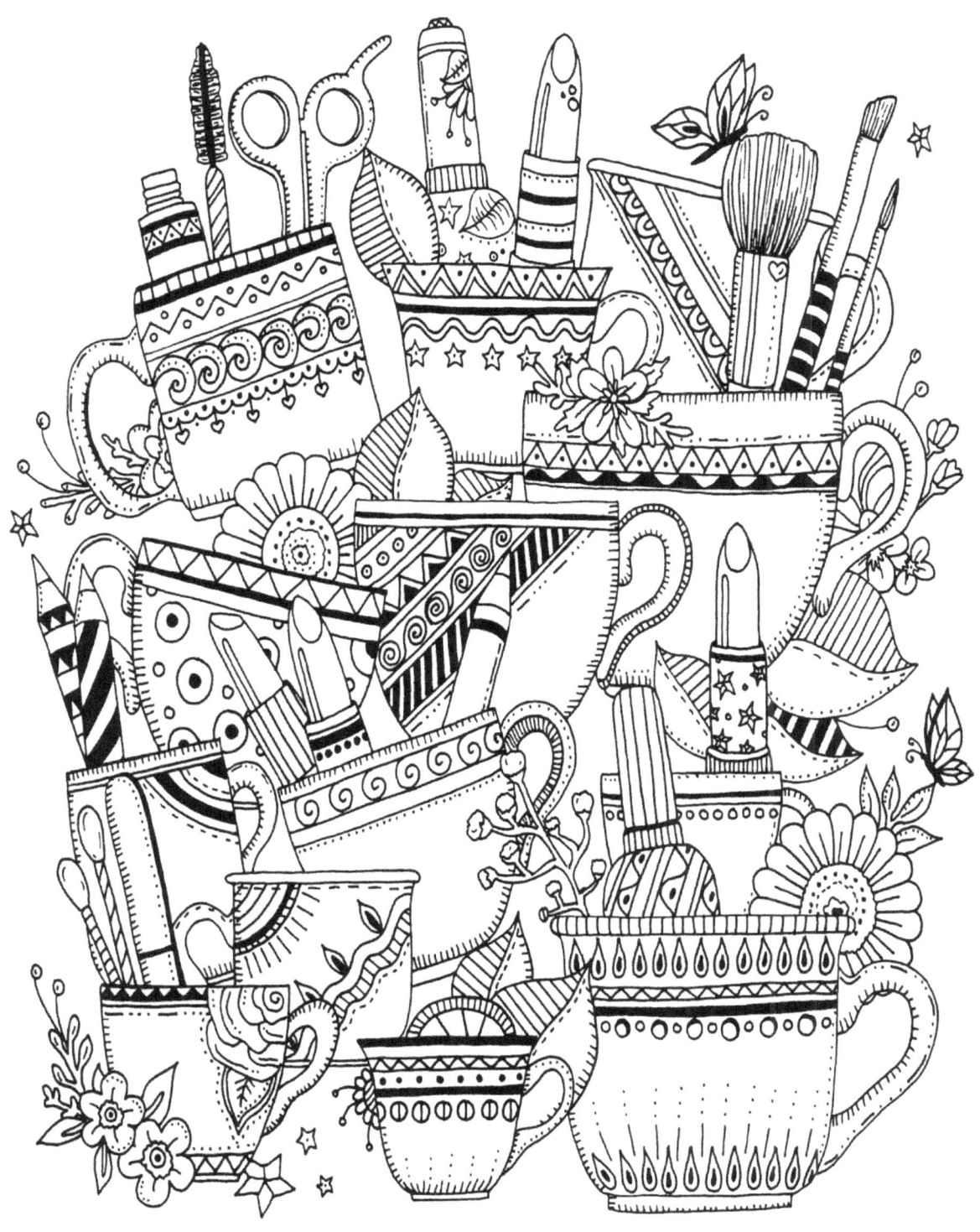

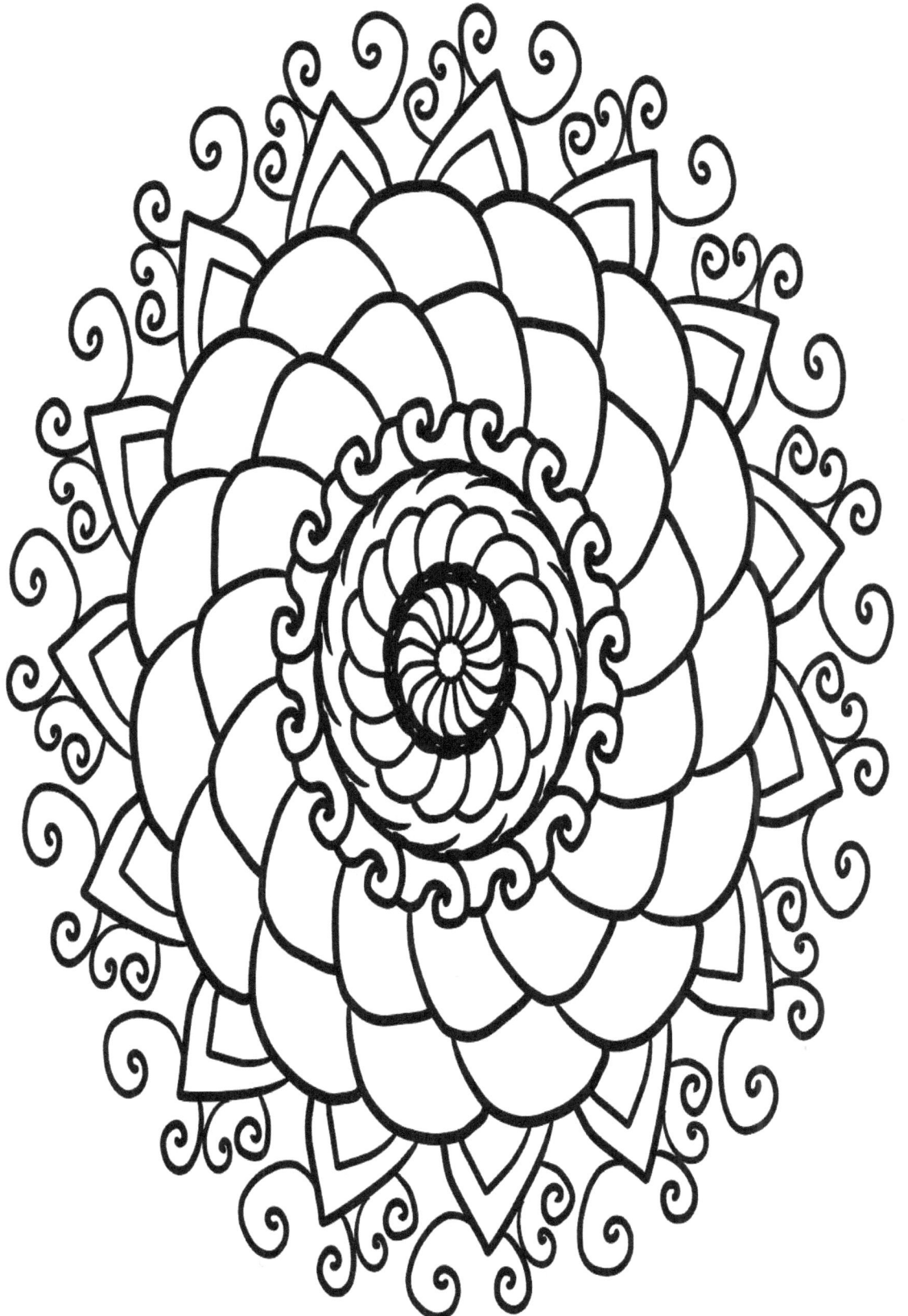

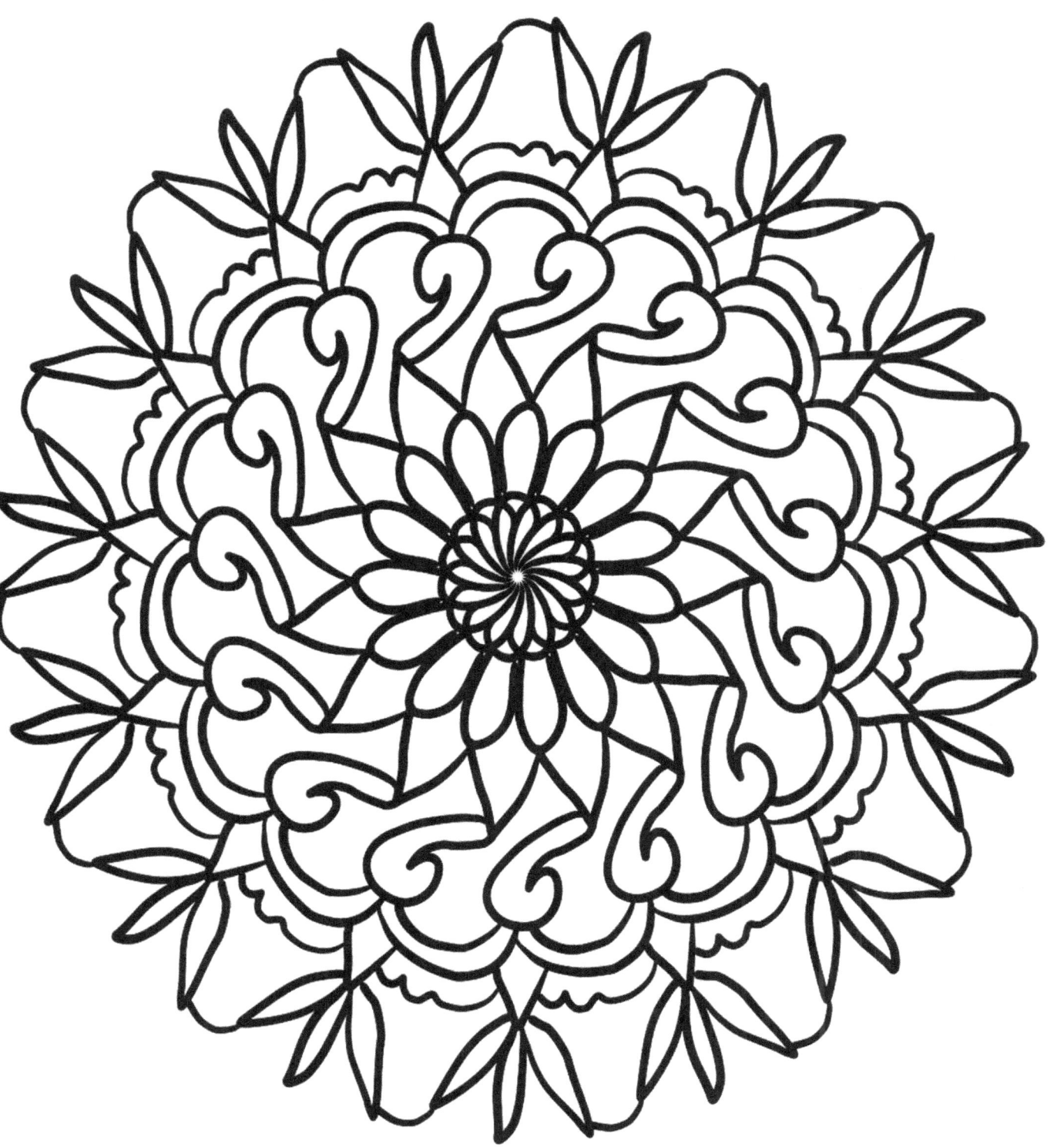

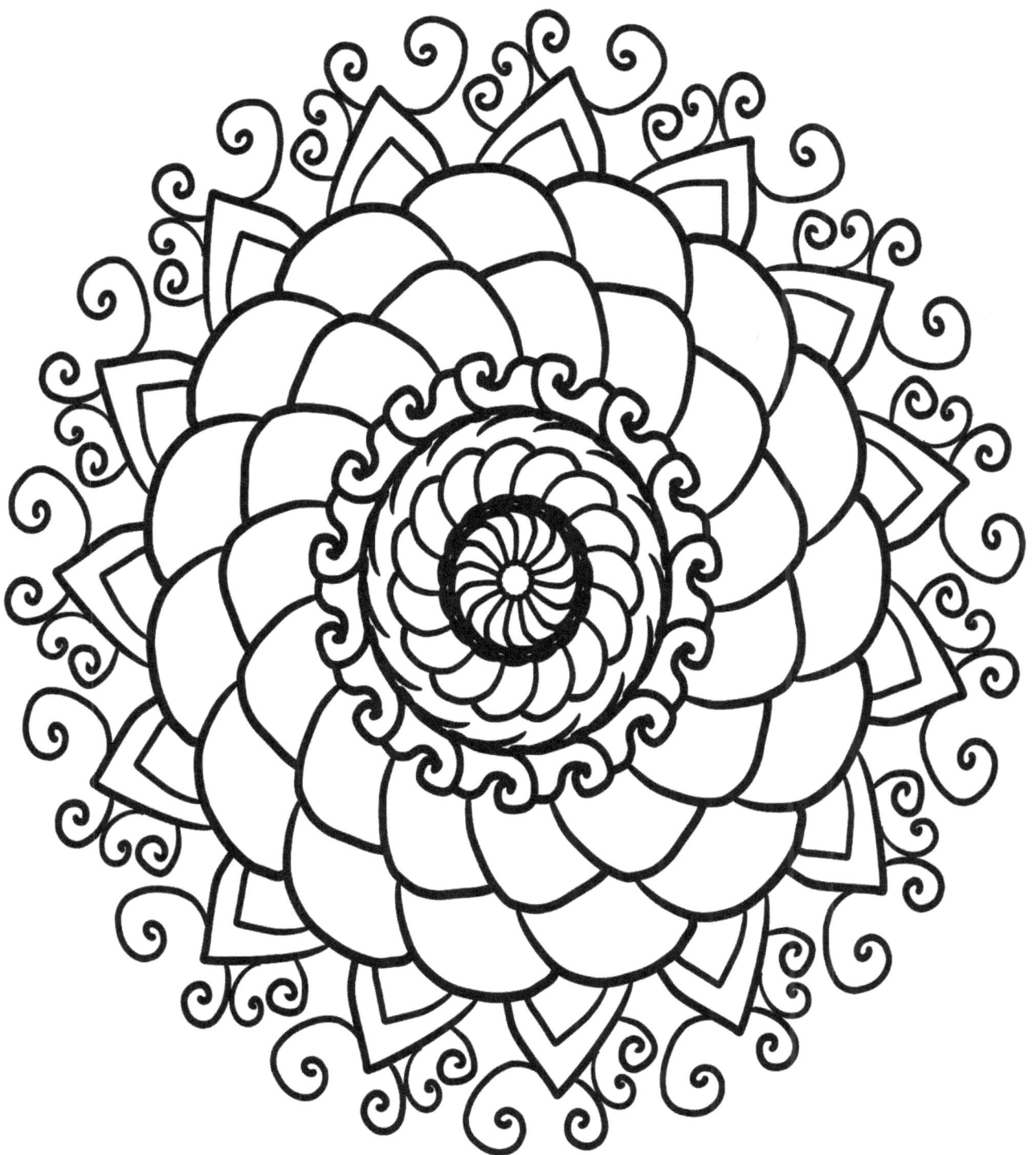

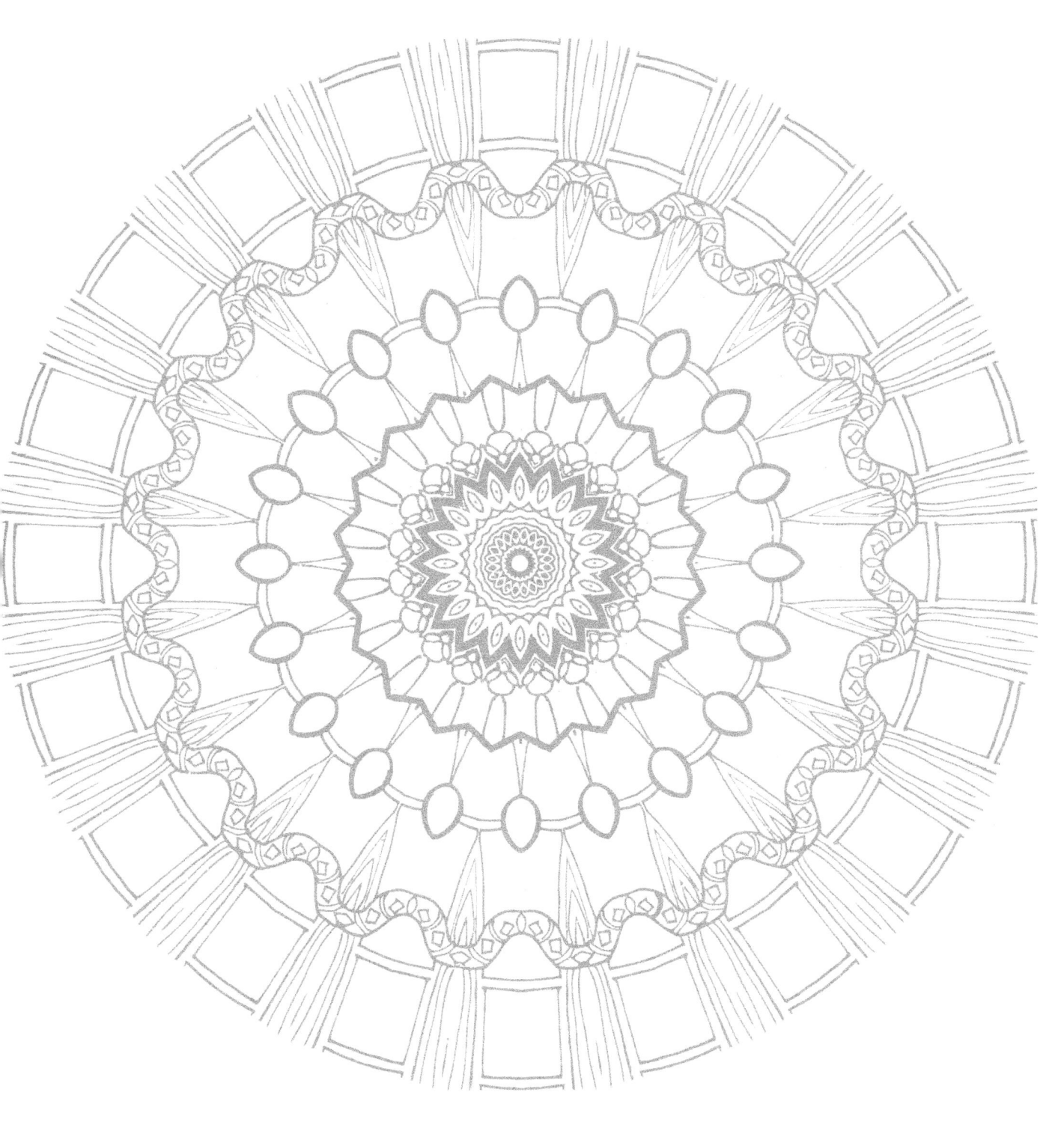

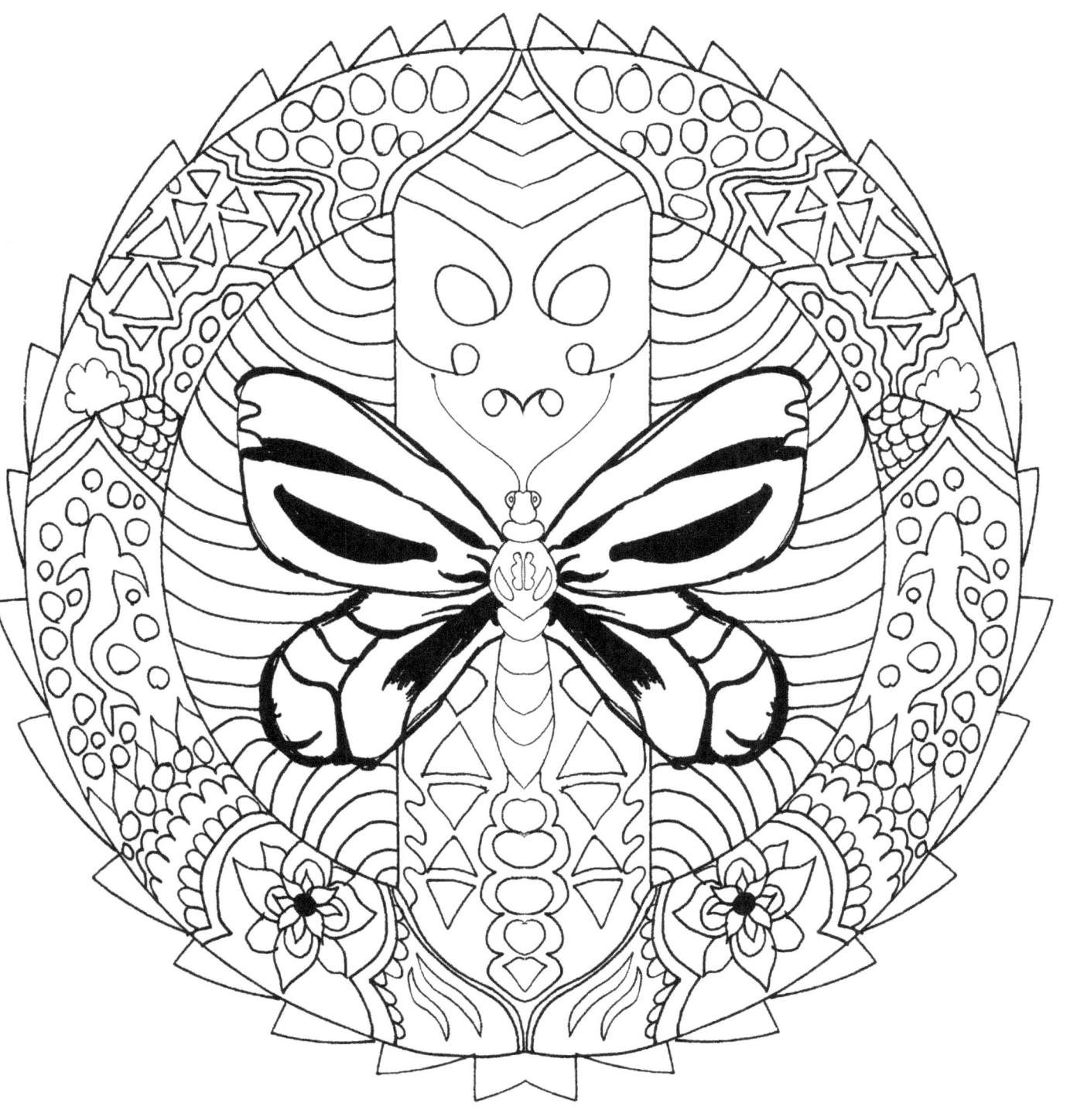

Organized Chaos

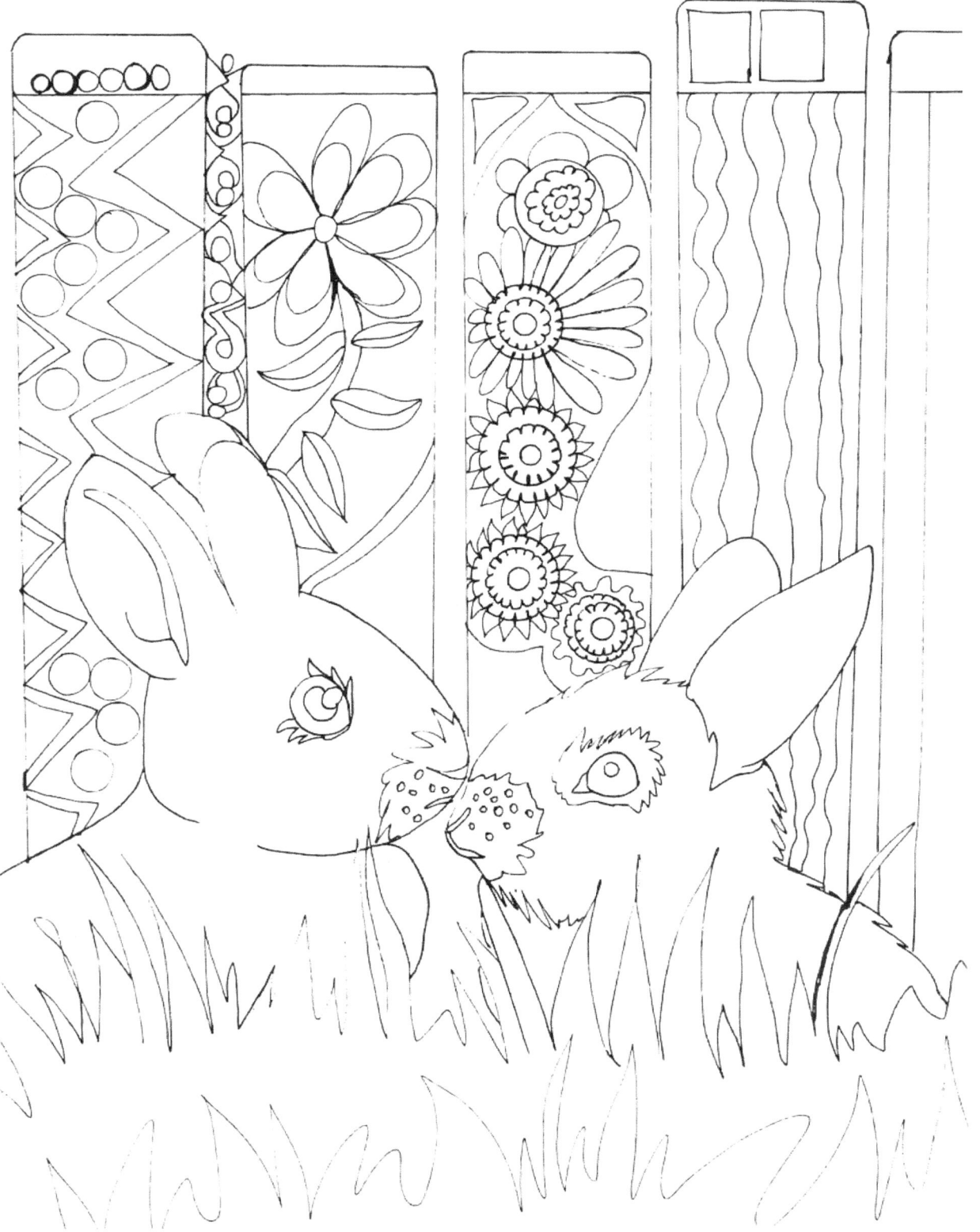

Organized Chaos

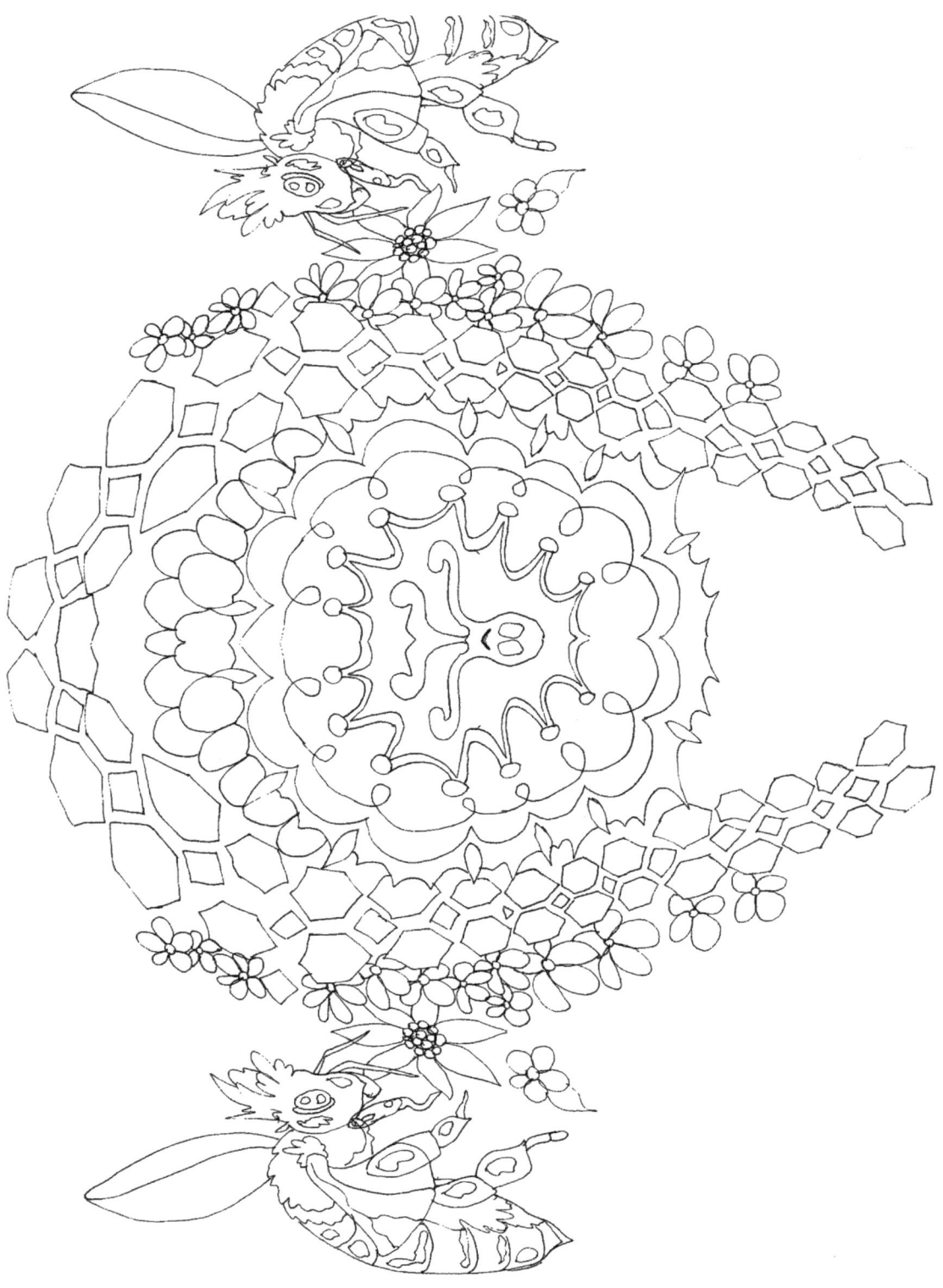

Organized Chaos

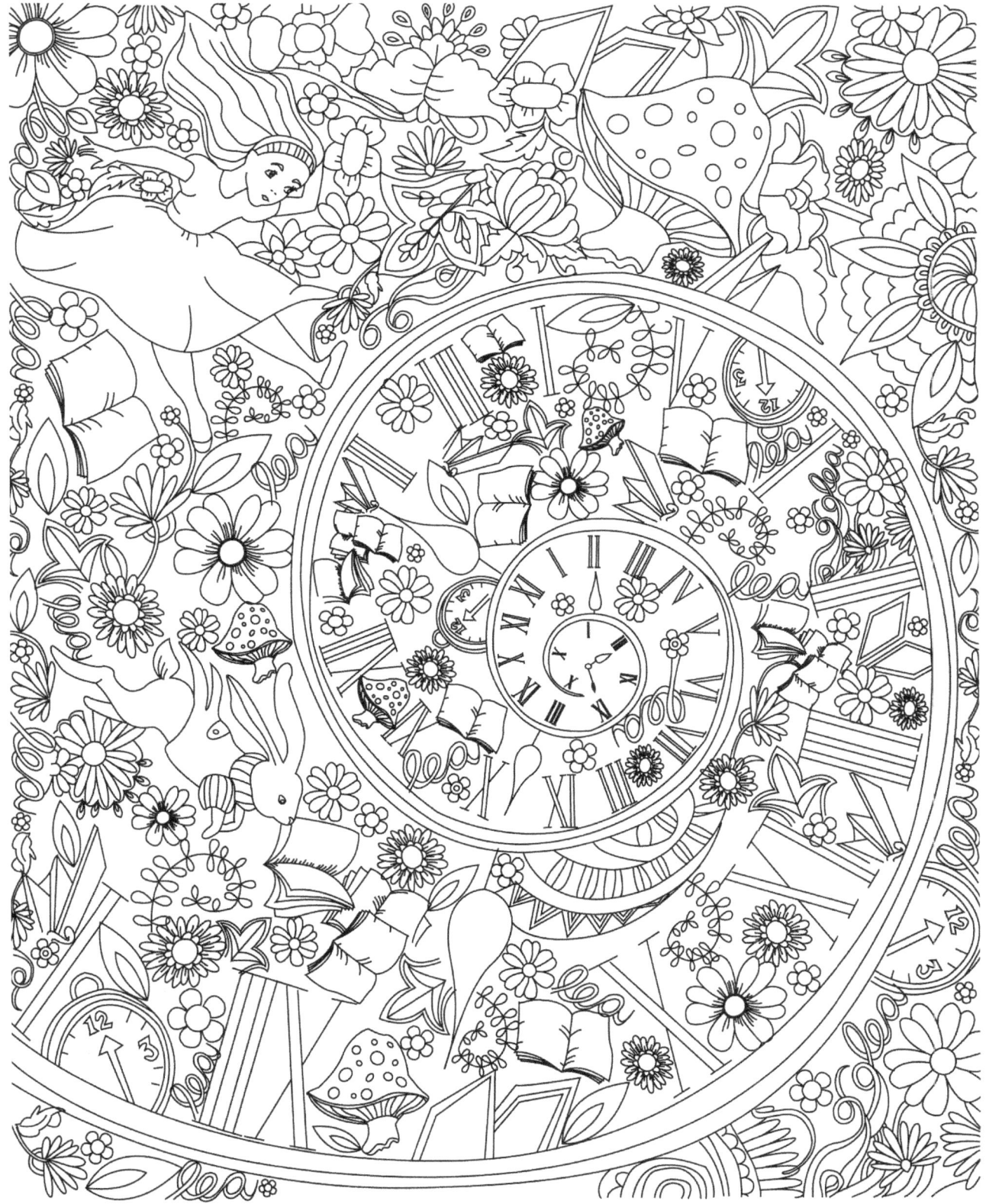

Organized Chaos

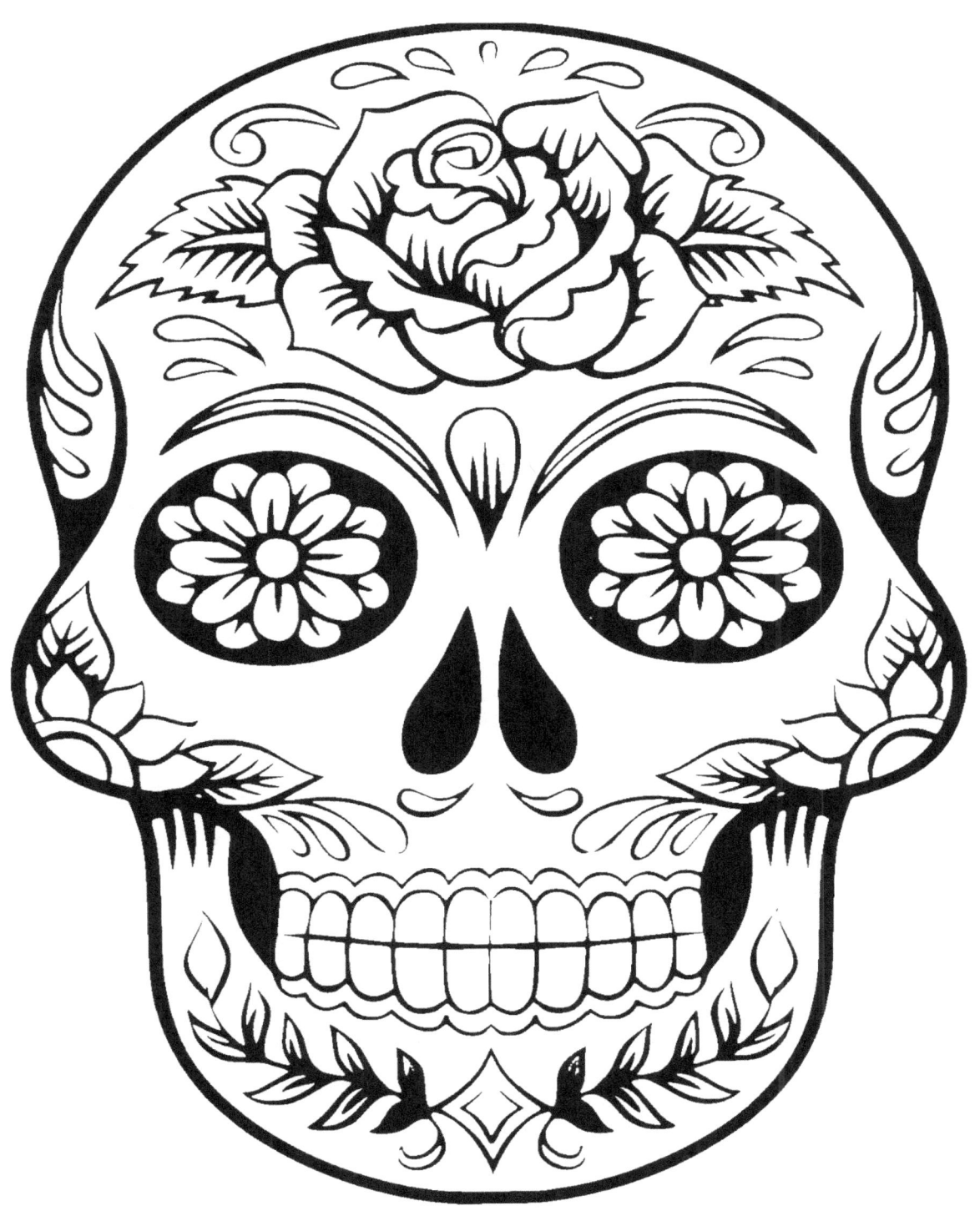

Organized Chaos

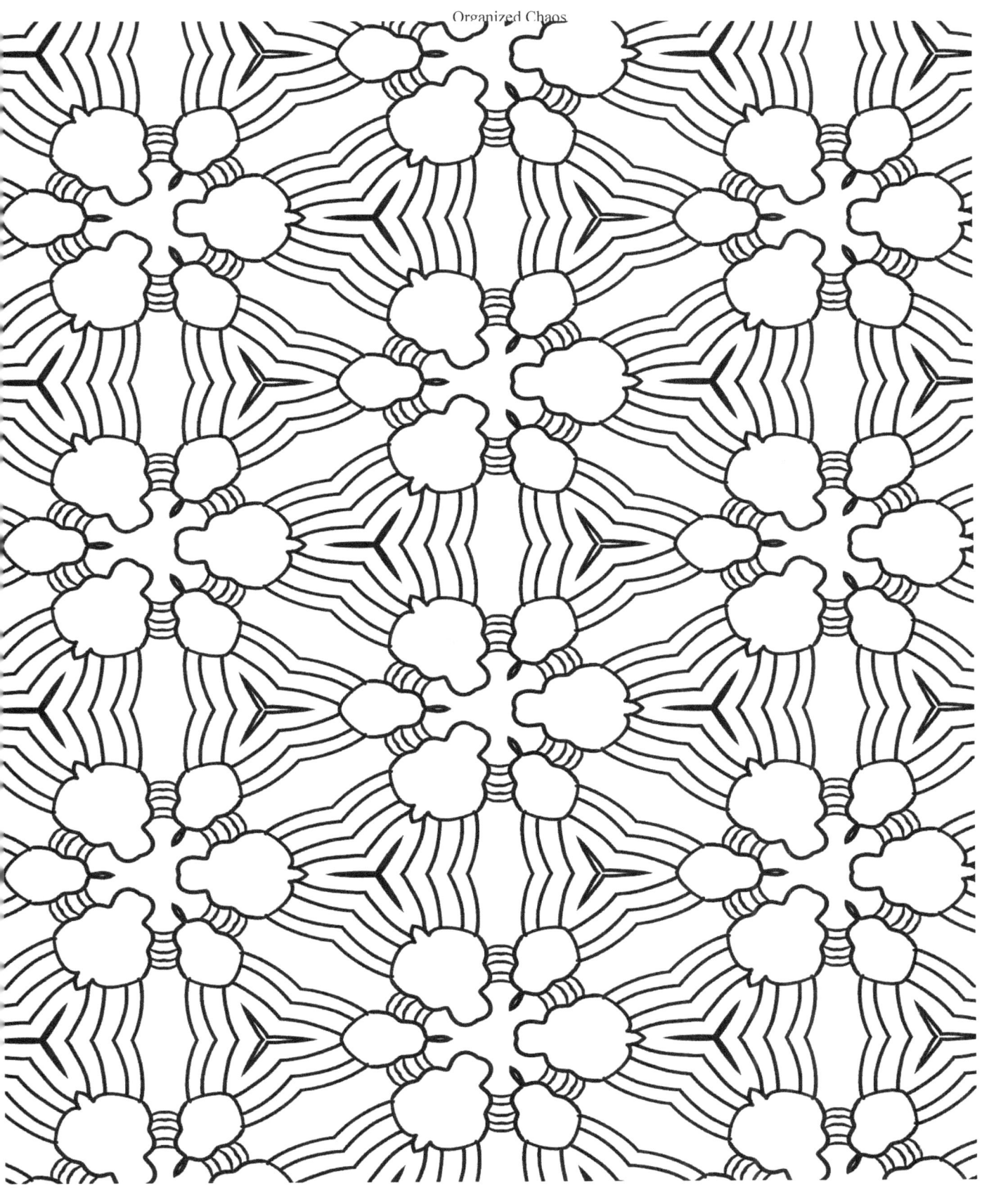

Organized Chaos

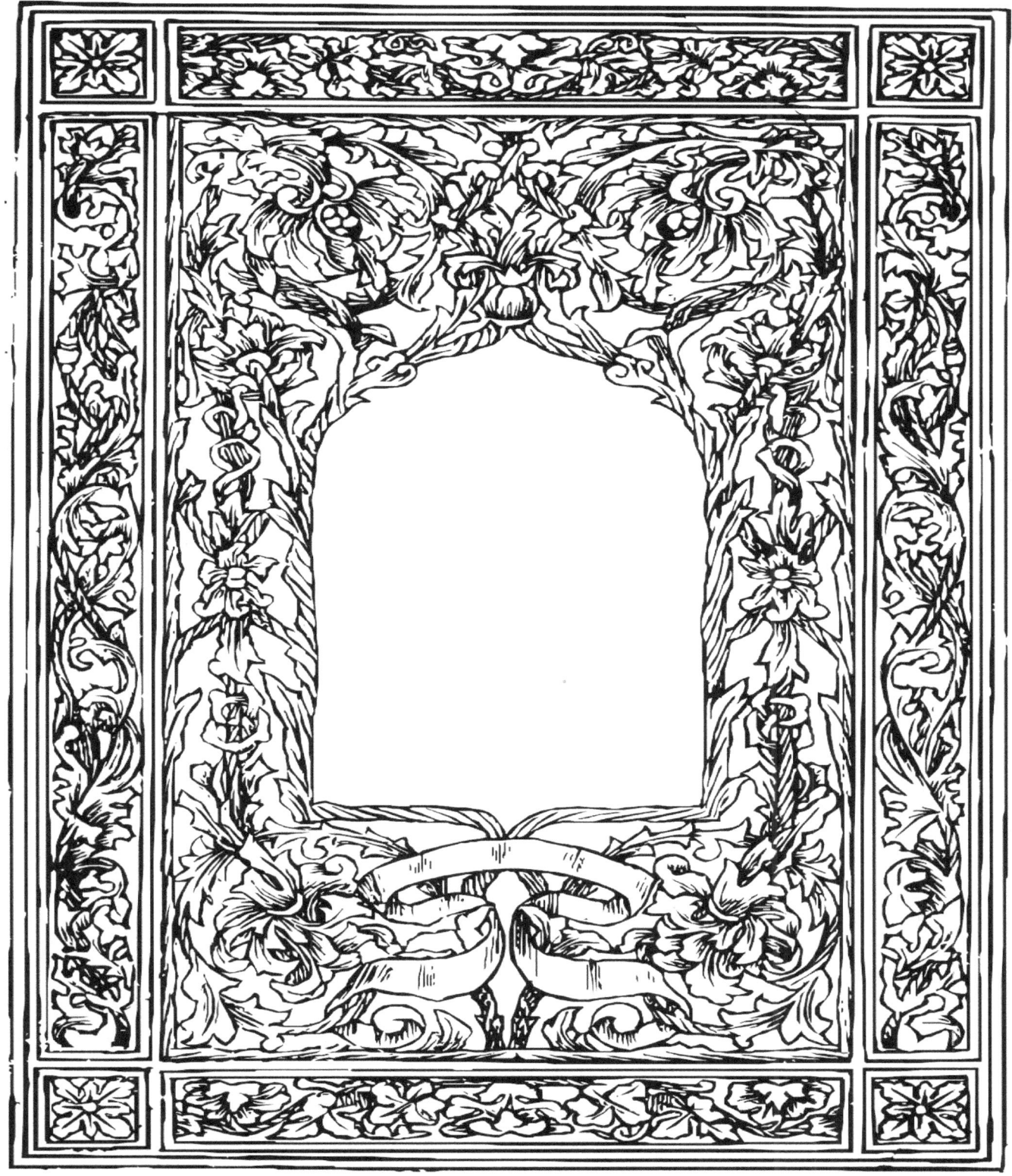

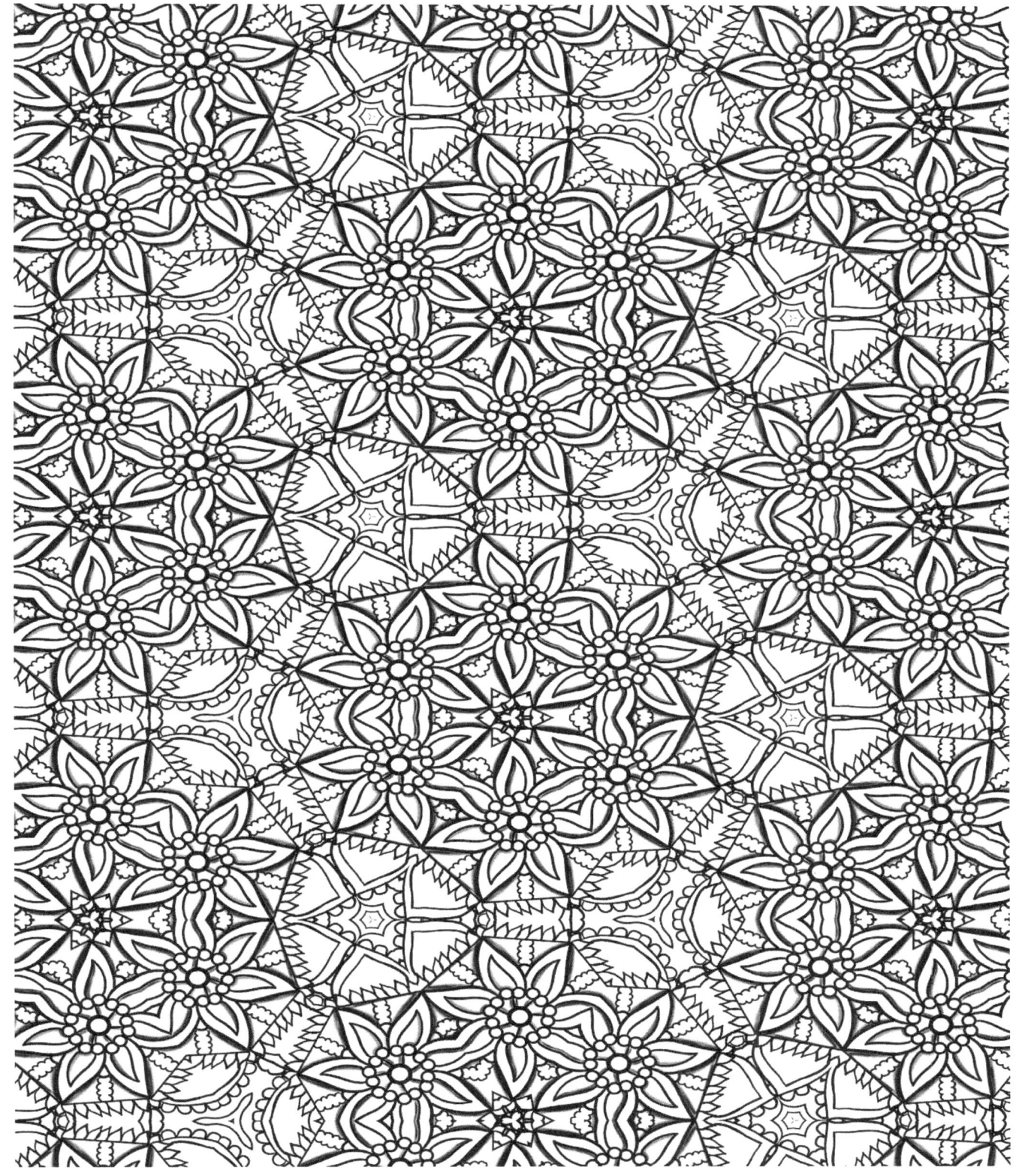

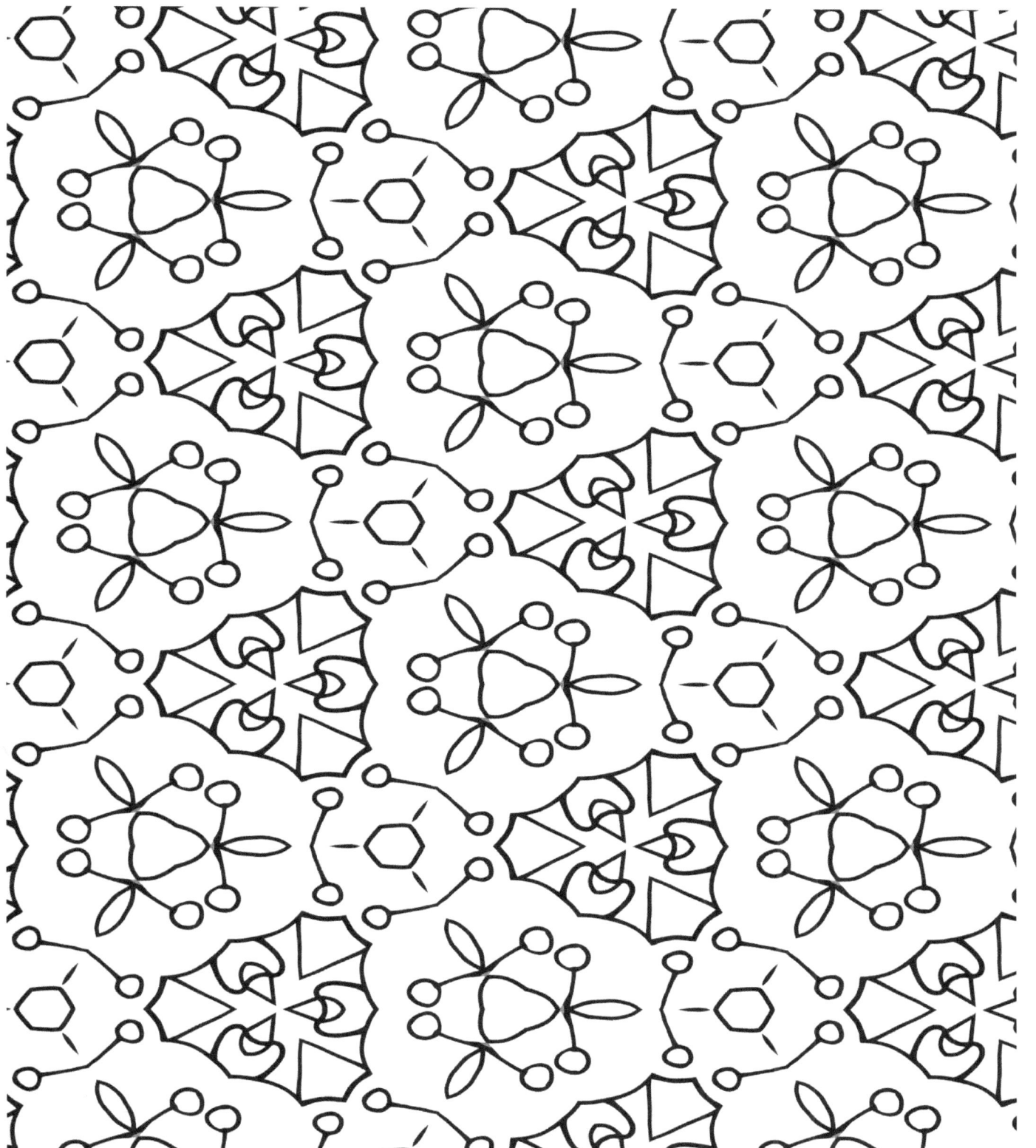

Organized Chaos

www.ingramcontent.com/pod-product-compliance
Lightning Source LLC
Chambersburg PA
CBHW082114220526
45472CB00009B/2172